DUMBARTON OAKS
CONFERENCE ON CHAVÍN

Chavín painted textile, Pre-Columbian Collection, PC.B.544,
Dumbarton Oaks Research Library and Collection, Washington, DC.

DUMBARTON OAKS CONFERENCE ON CHAVÍN

OCTOBER 26TH AND 27TH, 1968

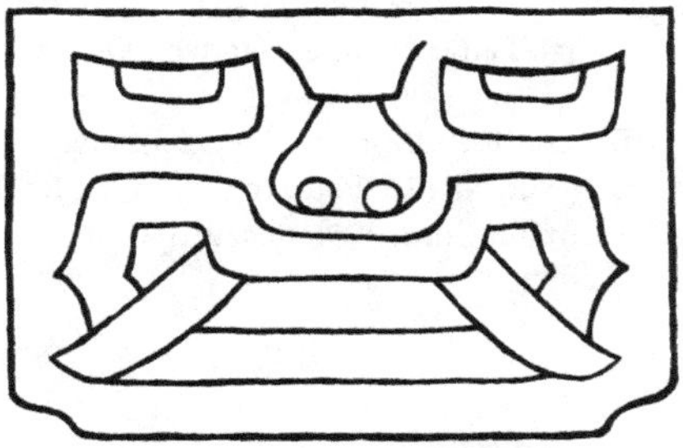

Elizabeth P. Benson, *Editor*

Dumbarton Oaks Research Library and Collection
TRUSTEES FOR HARVARD UNIVERSITY
Washington, DC

ISBN-13: 978-0-88402-037-0 [hardcover]
ISBN-13: 978-0-88402-455-2 [paperback]
Library of Congress catalog number 73-153502
LCCN permalink: https://lccn.loc.gov/73153502

Manufactured in the United States of America by
Sheridan Books, Inc., 450 Fame Avenue, Hanover, PA 17331 | (717) 632-3535

EU GPSR Authorised Representative
LOGOS EUROPE, 9 rue Nicolas Poussin, 17000, La Rochelle, France
E-mail: Contact@logoseurope.eu

Preface

THIS volume records the Conference on Chavín held at Dumbarton Oaks on October 26th and 27th, 1968, under the chairmanship of Junius Bird of the American Museum of Natural History. The first paper of the conference was presented by Hernán Amat Olazával and described the recent work at Chavín carried on by Dr. Amat and Luís Guillermo Lumbreras, under the sponsorship of the Corporación del Santa. Unfortunately, Dr. Amat's paper was not made available for this publication. We have substituted a brief report by Dr. Lumbreras, taken and translated from the magazine *Amaru*. The illustrations following this article were provided by Dr. Amat.

The other papers in the conference were concerned with either the possible origins of Chavín civilization or its spread to other regions. Chavín, the earliest civilization in Peru, with its great ceremonial center in the northern highlands, spread to the north coast and as far south as the Nasca Valley. Its influence is clear, but its origins are unknown, as is the nature of its diffusion. It was as an attempt to expand knowledge of these subjects that we planned this conference. The choice of Chavín as a subject seemed particularly appropriate because the first Dumbarton Oaks Pre-Columbian conference, a year earlier, concerned the Olmec, the contemporaneous early civilization in Mexico.

The Conference on Chavín was planned with a small group of speakers and a small audience limited to people particularly concerned with early Andean studies. At the Sunday morning session, following the planned Saturday program which this volume represents, papers were volunteered by Alan Sawyer, Gary Vescelius, and R. T. Zuidema.

We are appreciative of the able direction of Junius Bird, which contributed greatly to the success of this conference. We are particularly grateful to John S. Thacher, the former Director of Dumbarton Oaks, under whose aegis these conferences came into being, to Thomas P. Baird, the Associate Director, whose assistance in all aspects of the conference was invaluable, and to Barbara Braun, the Assistant Curator for the Pre-Columbian Collection, who helped make the conference possible, who worked on the editing of this publication, and who translated the Lumbreras paper. We are also greatly indebted to the staff of Dumbarton Oaks for their help in the presentation of the conference, particularly Mrs. Penelope Feuillan, who assisted the Pre-Columbian Collection.

ELIZABETH P. BENSON
MICHAEL D. COE

THE PANEL

Junius B. Bird, *Chairman*
Hernán Amat Olazával
Seiichi Izumi
Donald W. Lathrap
Thomas C. Patterson
John H. Rowe

THE PARTICIPANTS

Michael D. Coe
Clifford Evans
Kent V. Flannery
Julie Jones
Michael Kan
Mary Elizabeth King
Frederick Landmann
Rosa Fung de Lanning
Richard S. MacNeish
Betty J. Meggers
Dorothy Menzel
Victor A. Nuñez Regueiro
Fred Olsen
Peter I. Porres
Alan R. Sawyer
Harry Scheele
Mary Elizabeth Smith
Robert Sonin
Donald E. Thompson
Gary S. Vescelius
Stephen Williams
R. T. Zuidema

Contents

A

B

Fig. 1 A. *East façade of the temple at Chavín de Huantar, showing the Black-and-White Portal.* B. *Steps leading from the Sunken Courtyard.*

Towards a Re-evaluation of Chavín[1]

LUÍS GUILLERMO LUMBRERAS

UNIVERSIDAD NACIONAL MAYOR DE SAN MARCOS

> . . . a large building of huge stone blocks very well wrought; it was a guaca, and one of the most famous of the heathen sanctuaries, like Rome or Jerusalem with us; the Indians used to come and make their offerings and sacrifices, for the Devil pronounced many oracles from here, and so they repaired here from all over the kingdom. There are large subterranean halls and apartments, and even accurate information that they extend under the river which flows by the guaca or ancient sanctuary.
>
> —A. Vázquez de Espinosa[2]

TODAY Chavín de Huantar is a beautiful rural village located at the entrance of the Callejón de Conchucos, on the eastern slopes of the Cordillera Blanca, more than 3,000 meters above sea level, at the confluence of two rivers of glacial origin, the larger of which, the Puchka, runs from the south to drain, many kilometers to the northeast, into the immense Marañón.

Almost three millennia ago it was a ceremonial center, to which people from a vast territory of the Andes surely flocked, as—according to the report of the chronicler Vázquez de Espinosa—they still did until shortly before the arrival of the Spanish.

The importance of this place was noted centuries ago by the Spanish chroniclers who visited it in the early years of the Colonial era and later by the travelers of the eighteenth and nineteenth centuries who were enthusiastic about the monumental aspect of the buildings and the beautiful decoration visible in the finely-cut stones. But its importance within the historical development of Peruvian society was first realized only in this century by the Peruvian archaeologist Julio C. Tello.

1. This article appeared in *Amaru; Revista de artes y ciencias* (April 1967), pp. 49–60, Lima. Photographs and drawings published here are courtesy of Hernán Amat Olazával. The drawings were made by Félix Caycho Q.

2. Antonio Vázquez de Espinosa, Compendium and Description of the West Indies (trans. by Charles Upson Clark), *Smithsonian Miscellaneous Collections, vol. 102, Publication 3646*, p. 491. Washington.

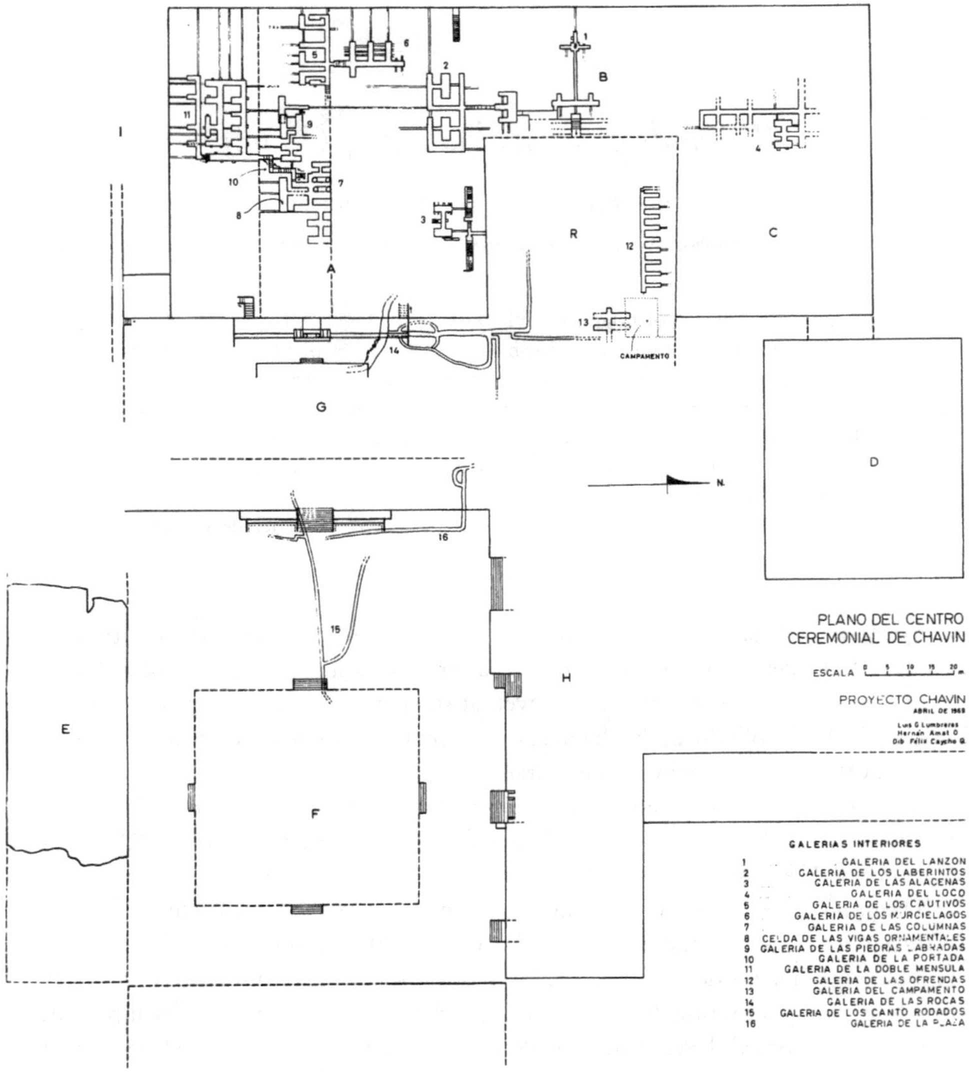

Fig. 2 *Plan of the ceremonial center at Chavín de Huantar.*

The name Chavín signifies, for Americanists, not only the ruins of Chavín de Huantar, but also a stage of Andean culture history in which are included dozens of ceremonial centers, villages, and simple farms, all of them very ancient. These were inhabited by agricultural people who consumed maize, made ceramics, worked gold, wove fine cloth of cotton or wool, and were bound to a religion whose deity was conceived as having feline attributes. For archaeologists, Chavín is a particular, unmistakable technology and art, which flourished in the Central Andes—in what today is called Peru—during the last millennium before our era.

In fact—and as Tello asserted—Chavín is a culture which spread to nearly all of Peru; the site occupied by the ruins of this name was probably the point of dispersion for most of its characteristic features. Tello based his initial theories on a stylistic analysis of the worked stones, on which are represented abundant and complex images; later, he discovered "black incised" ware, which from that time on (1934) became the basic criterion for identification of the Chavín culture. Certainly, an excess of generalization led Tello, and many other archaeologists, to label as Chavín all black incised ceramics made in the Andes. Wisely, A. L. Kroeber suggested the term "chavinoid" (resembling Chavín), and this has been applied in the past few years to the cultures whose ceramics have some similarity to those found by Tello at Chavín.

Subsequent work permits us to further refine the characteristics of Chavín, and only in the last couple of years have archaeologists begun to be concerned with pre-Chavín and non-Chavín complexes by addressing themselves to those chavinoid materials whose traits do not fit in with the Chavín style proper. But the curious thing in recent years has been that, inasmuch as the few potsherds that Tello found in the ruins of Chavín de Huantar in 1934 had been only partially sorted out, archaeologists took as an archetype of the culture a coastal form that its discoverer, Rafael Larco Hoyle, had christened Cupisnique. All those that were similar to Cupisnique could be called chavinoid; Tello himself, in order to illustrate Chavín ceramics, had to resort in various of his publications to the beautiful bottles in the Cupisnique style characteristic of the Chicama Valley, on the north coast.

Recently, under the direction of Hernán Amat and the author, the work of exploring the ruins of Chavín de Huantar has been reinitiated and the results of the first season have been highly satisfactory. Part of the architectural history of the immense ceremonial center as well as several of the ceramic phases have been observed, and have served as an important point of departure for a re-evaluation of this enormous complex which archaeologists know by the name Chavín.

THE TEMPLE

The currently visible buildings of Chavín de Huantar are the fruit of the efforts of many men during several centuries; in what today appears as an asymmetrical system of pyramids, plazas, and platforms (Figs. 1 and 2), one discovers the superposition of constructions of several epochs which have endured the destruction, remodeling, and modification appropriate to a place with a millennium-long history. The oldest temple thus far identified is horseshoe-shaped; at its center stood the sacred stone image of the

Fig. 3 *Construction in the old temple at Chavín de Huantar. A and B show the Lanzón.*

Fig. 4 *Galleries in the temple at Chavín de Huantar, showing various types of masonry.*

anthropomorphic feline divinity, carved in the form of a knife and therefore given the name Lanzón (Fig. 3). Subsequently, the inhabitants decided that this east-oriented temple was too small, and added to the wings, thus extending the structure in the north and south directions. In a third epoch, they abandoned the original plan and erected in the southern part of the temple a pyramid of quadrangular plan, which shifted the central focus away from the old temple associated with Lanzón and to a portal decorated with images of falcon-like birds. In an even later epoch, they erected a small pyramid in the north section of the ceremonial center, but this must have taken place when Chavín de Huantar had already clearly entered into a period of decadence. Still later, when other people occupied the site, the temples were not abandoned, although the buildings were partially destroyed and the sacred places covered with the refuse of their domestic habitations. The barbarians who invaded Chavín de Huantar made their houses all around the pyramids and interred their dead there; the subterranean galleries were desecrated and used as collective mausoleums. What Tello (1960) considered rubbish from the destruction of the pyramids through natural action, is in reality the evidence of several centuries of reoccupation of the site by new people. The Incas were familiar with the "adoratorio" of Chavín de Huantar, and it is probable that in that epoch the houses of the new occupants were more visible than the old temples which have only now reappeared, thanks to the work of the archaeologists.

It is not correct to say that the architecture of Chavín de Huantar represents a unity (Figs. 3–5); nevertheless, there are formal aspects which are sustained over the entire length of the Chavín period. As a whole, the buildings appear to have been built in conformity with a uniform system, so that they have come to be considered contemporaneous. Their appearance, from the exterior, is that of truncated pyramids of one or two massive platforms whose highest point must be over ten meters. But the Chavín de Huantar pyramids are not like others known in the Andes; their interior is formed by a network of galleries on different levels composed of passages, cells, ramps, and storerooms, which receive ventilation through one of the ducts of quadrangular section which connect the interior with the exterior. In one of these galleries, in the old temple, one finds the divine image of the Lanzón, and in another gallery—called that of the Vigas Ornamentales—there are carved on the stone beams of the ceiling images of a fish and a crustacean, surely related forms prescribed by the cult.

In the first epoch it appears that more than one type of gallery was constructed in the temple; behind the building one finds the Galería de las Rocas, whose surfaces were made from river stones, while the galleries of the temple itself consist of stones cut in the form of parallelepipeds. In the Rocas have been found the most ancient Chavín ceramics now known. In later times—in the second epoch—the surfaces consisted, in some cases, of finely cut and polished stones.

Fig. 5 (left) *The Black-and-White Portal.* (right) *Entrance to the Galería de la Portada.*

The architectural differences of the various epochs of Chavín are not yet very clear, but some have great importance. In the first epoch, the exterior surface of the horseshoe-shaped pyramid was made with large and small cut stones placed in alternating rows; the surfaces of the second and third epochs, on the other hand, show an alternation of large and small stones within each row.

THE STYLE

We have said that the name Chavín refers more to a culture than to a site; in reality, it refers to an artistic style. In a surprising quantity of stones or cut slabs (commonly called "stelae") which function as cornices, lintels, corbels, tablets, etc., in some other large stones in the form of obelisks, and in other Chavín-style objects of stone, bone, shell, etc., one notes a great variety of cult images elaborated according to traditional artistic conventions. In conformity with these conventions, the personages are represented in a metaphorical language, their corporeal elements functioning as symbols of the most diverse origin and significance. One cannot say that all the representations correspond to deities, but certainly all are connected in some way with the forces which, according to the beliefs of that time, rule over nature. Within this complicated system of representation, the feline, the bird, and the serpent contribute the fundamental elements out of which the anthropomorphic forms of the most important personages are composed. The feline appears related to the jaguar, the bird to the falcon family, and perhaps to the condor, and the serpent to the *amaru*. Fish, marine shells, plants, owls, and other animals always appear on a secondary level.

They did not always manage to translate the style of the carved stones to other materials, and only exceptionally does one encounter it in its original mode outside of Chavín de Huantar itself. It could be copied best in small objects of bone, stone, or shell; the ceramics, on the other hand, almost always exhibited, outside of Chavín de Huantar, an epigonal aspect of the style. Such was the case in Cupisnique, in Ancón, in Kuntur Wasi, etc., owing to the fact that Chavín pottery has its own stylistic elements which always functioned as the taxonomic foundation of the style. There are, without doubt, some common elements among the different media, for example, the upward-looking pupil and the thick-lipped mouth in the form of a U, generally with curved fangs. These traits have also permitted the identification of the style on painted fabrics and pyroengraved gourds.

THE CERAMICS

As noted above, the ceramics of Chavín (Fig. 6) have almost always been identified and classified on the basis of the ceramics of the Chicama Valley, which Larco called Cupisnique. Thanks to the work which we have carried out in the ancient sanctuary, we

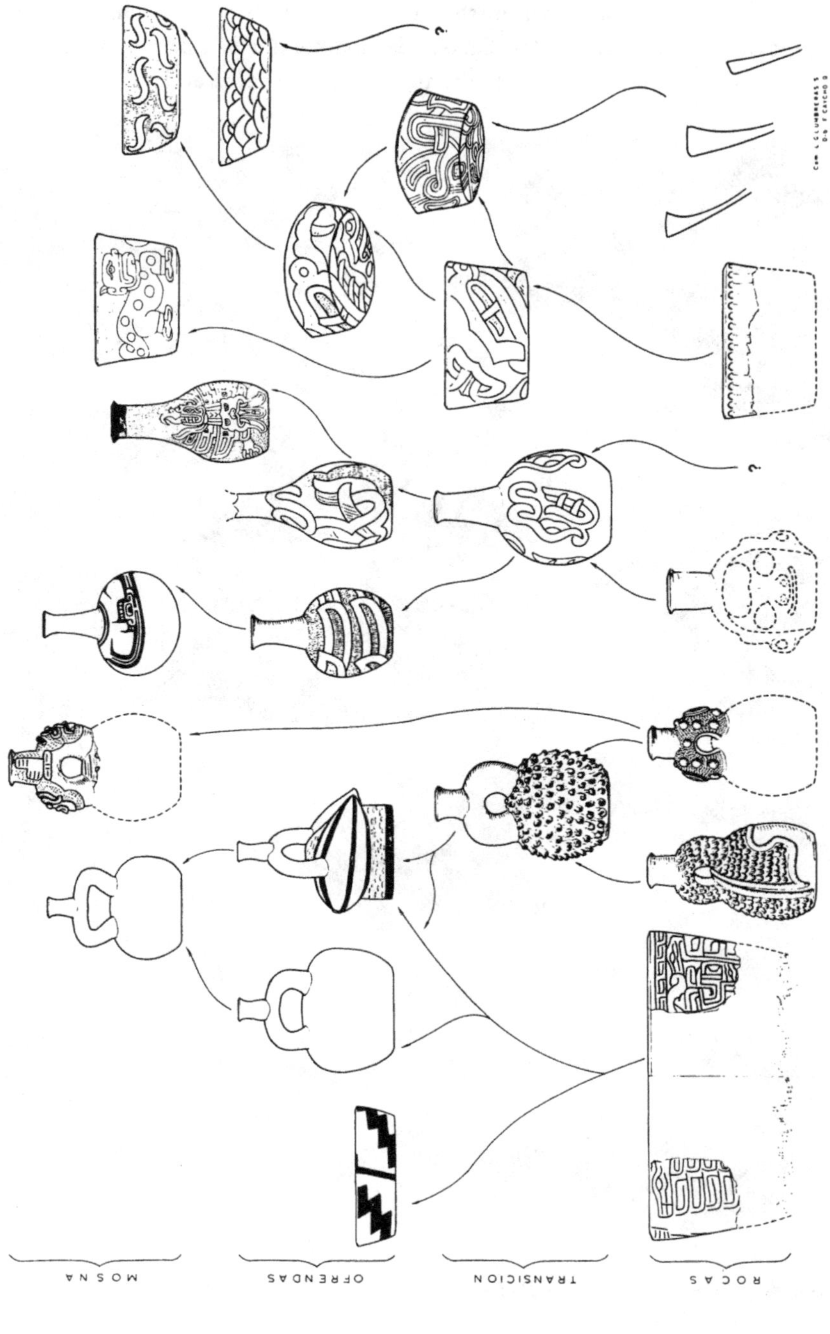

Fig. 6 *Chart depicting the evolution of Chavín ceramics.*

now know that Cupisnique is no more than a regional variation of the Chavín style, conforming to the influences exerted by Chavín de Huantar during a certain period of time. Larco Hoyle (1941), in excavating the cemeteries of Barbacoa and Sausal, in the Chi-

Fig. 7 *Sherds of Rocas Fine Black and Polished Gray pottery.*

cama Valley, discovered a complex of tombs associated with a ceremonial pottery with some stylistic elements related to Chavín, which he named "nepeñanos" in the belief that the origin of the style lay in the Nepeña Valley. Unfortunately, Larco Hoyle died precisely when he was going to discuss with us our latest finds, preventing us from knowing his valued interpretation.

Fig. 8 *Sherds of Rocas Polished Gray pottery.*

Fig. 9 *Sherds of Rocas Incised Red and Polished Gray pottery.*

In Chavín, we have thus far been able to recover, in a verified association, two types of ceremonial ceramics in deposits in the Rocas and Ofrendas galleries.

The Rocas ceramics (Figs. 7–9) have a solid appearance, similar to stone. The largest group is represented by vases of gray or black color with incised, engraved, or modeled decoration, to which are added the fine engraved, polished, and dentate ornamentation, and other forms of surface finish which make for contrast in the plane areas. Among the fragments of this type that have been found thus far, the representation of a feline head done in relief on the stirrup spout of a bottle is of special interest. The most notable forms are bottles with globular bodies with a small but thick stirrup spout, and bowls with vertical walls and beveled borders generally thicker than the walls. The spouts of the pitchers and bottles usually end in a prominent flange.

Together with the gray pottery there are pieces of red pottery with broad incised designs whose incisions have been filled with a black pigment with a graphite base; some gray pieces also display a similar treatment. The red pottery of this type is, in all known cases, related to large bowls decorated inside as well as outside; one of these shows the image of a falcon-like bird with extended wings.

Of the Ofrendas ceramics we possess a considerable number of pieces, almost entirely restored, in the Museum of Archaeology of the University of San Marcos; hence our information is abundant. The collection recovered from Ofrendas does not show a single style and probably, notwithstanding the association, does not correspond to a single moment in the history of Chavín. We have until now managed to distinguish four groups, which we call Ofrendas, Negro Fino, Wacheqsa, and Mosna. The Ofrendas group (Figs. 10–23) is the most widespread and undoubtedly represents a uniform style in which the central image is a personage with an enlarged head, with only two upper fangs visible. It might have been based on the image which appears in the obelisk found in Chavín and brought to the Museum of San Marcos by Dr. Tello in 1919, and therefore known as the "Tello Obelisk."

Ofrendas pottery is extremely fine; one of its types, that which we know as Caramelo (for the color of the pieces), shows a finish resembling that of porcelain, with relief decoration alternating with incision. The predominant forms are: 1) bottles with elongated spouts, globular bodies, and flat bases and 2) bowls with walls which are almost always divergent, and flat or rounded bases.

The group called Negro Fino has only been provisionally separated. Through its decoration, it has greater continuity with the style of the stones. Stylistic considerations suggest that it should be later than Ofrendas, but they do not exclude its contemporaneity. The forms appear to be basically the same as those of Ofrendas. Here, the motifs represented are the feline and the falcon, both having the same stylistic treatment as the stones of the portal of the third epoch.

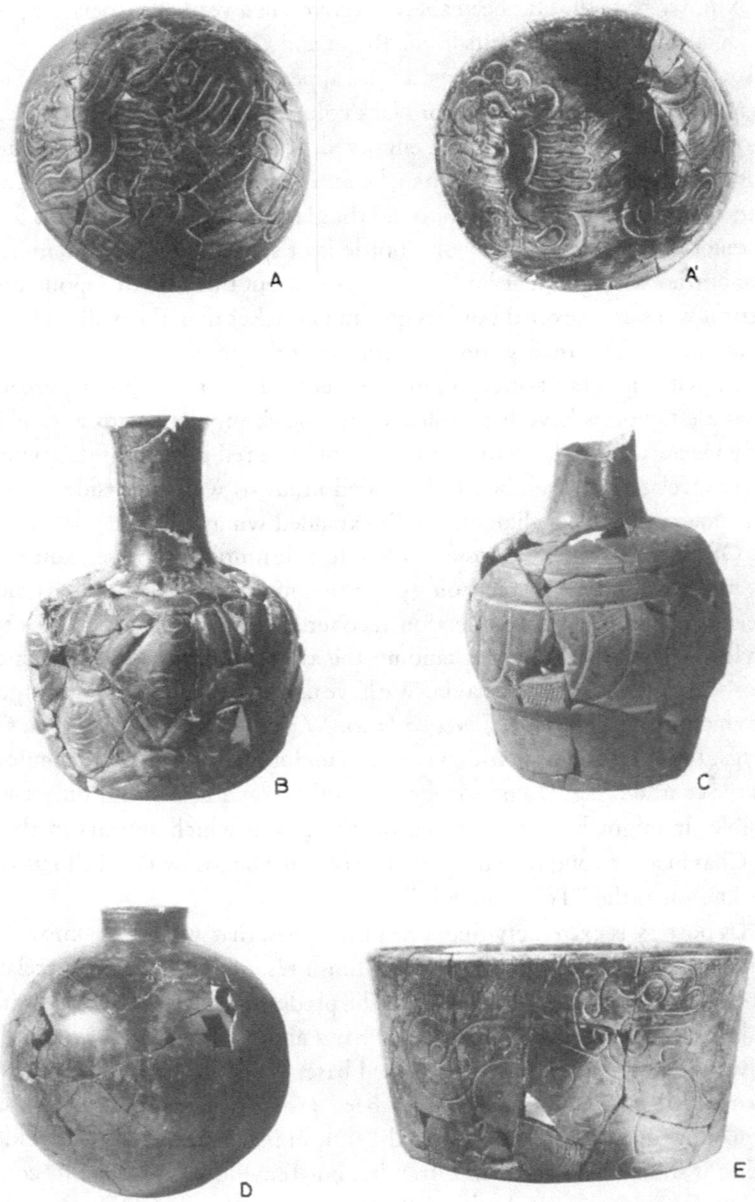

Fig. 10 *Pottery from the Ofrendas gallery, Negro Fino and Ofrendas Polished Gray.*

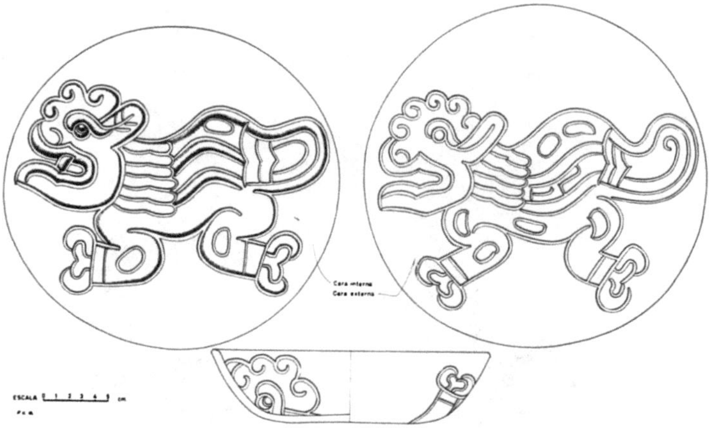

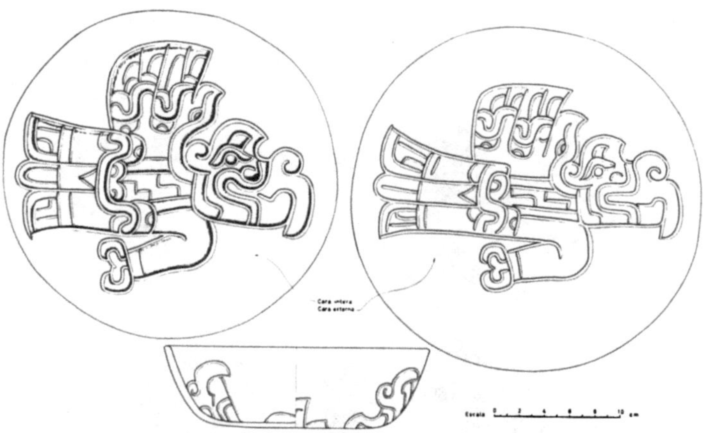

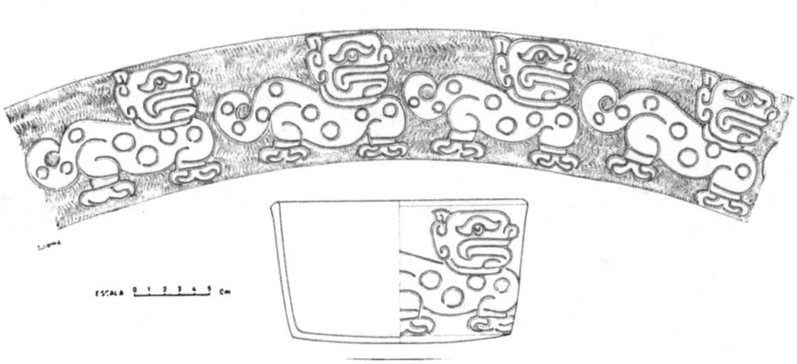

Fig. 11 (above) *Ofrendas Polished Gray bowl (Fig. 10A), showing inner and outer faces with a (winged?) feline.*

Fig. 12 (center) *Ofrendas Polished Gray bowl that makes a pair with Fig. 11.*

Fig. 13 (below) *Negro Fino bowl (Fig. 10E) from the Ofrendas gallery, with repetitions of a naturalistic feline.*

Fig. 14 *Various types of pottery from the Ofrendas gallery.*

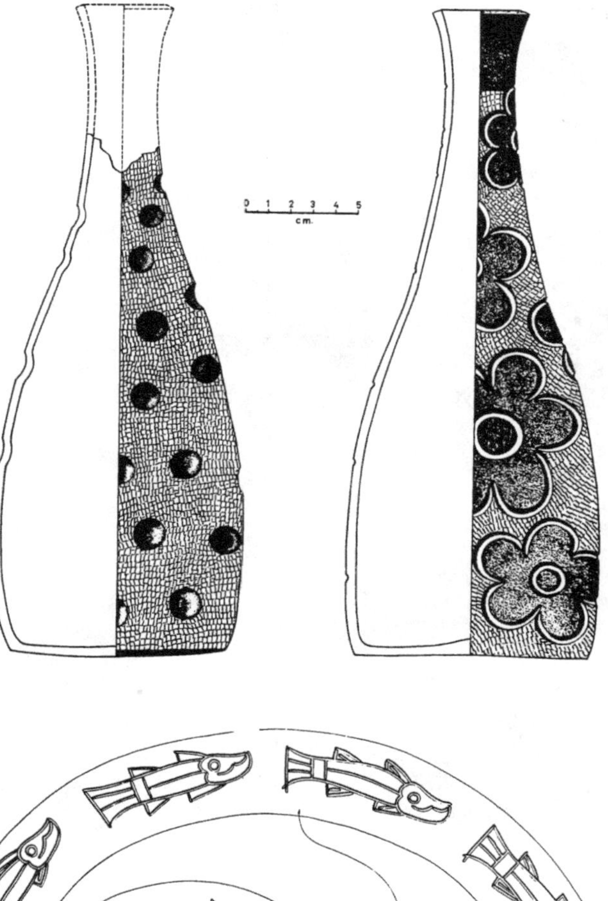

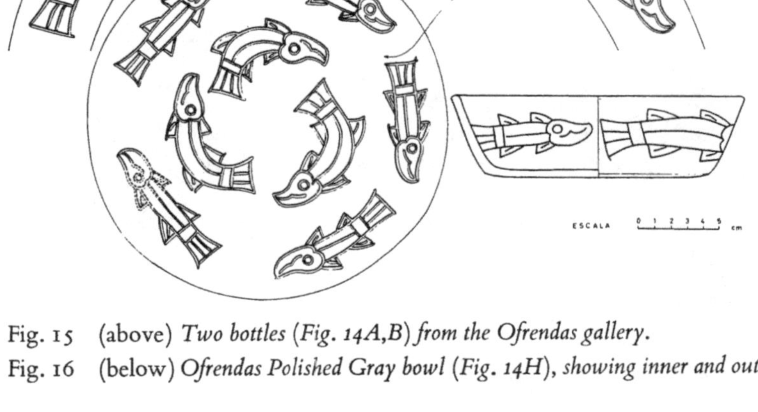

Fig. 15 (above) *Two bottles (Fig. 14A,B) from the Ofrendas gallery.*

Fig. 16 (below) *Ofrendas Polished Gray bowl (Fig. 14H), showing inner and outer faces.*

Fig. 17 *Bottles and bowls found in the Ofrendas gallery.*

Fig. 18 (above) *Bottle (Fig. 17A) of atypical shape and design from the Ofrendas gallery. The monster is reminiscent of the Paracas style.*

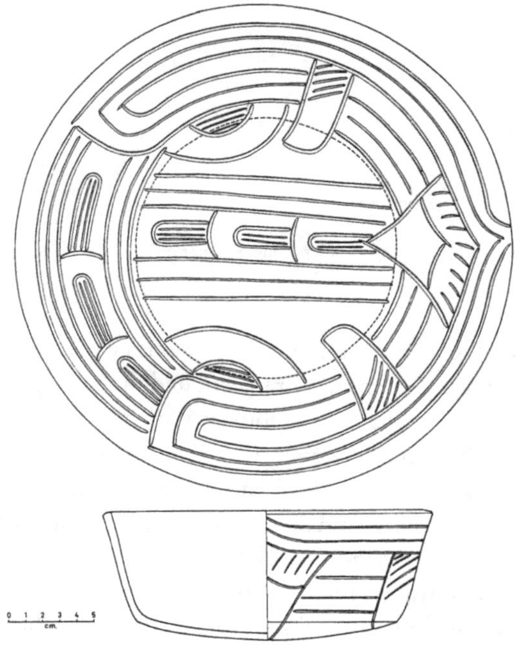

Fig. 19 (left) *Bowl (Fig. 17F) with the Ofrendas monster.*

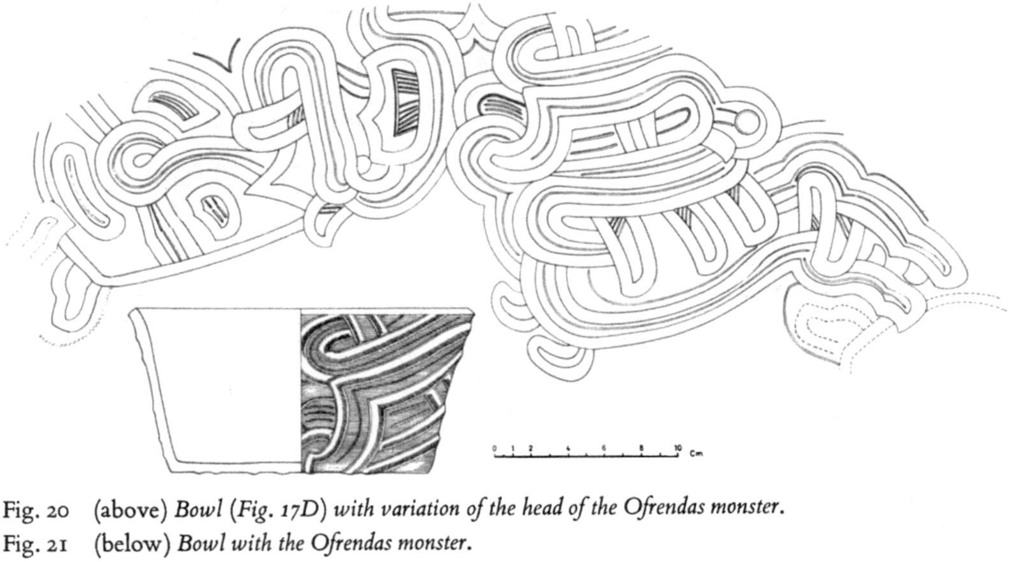

Fig. 20 (above) *Bowl (Fig. 17D) with variation of the head of the Ofrendas monster.*
Fig. 21 (below) *Bowl with the Ofrendas monster.*

The Wacheqsa style (Fig. 24), on the other hand, is rather different. It is characterized by the predominance of red ceramics, which, when they are decorated, have graphite filling the areas of the design. In contrast to the Rocas pottery with graphite, the Wacheqsa incisions are not painted, and they are, moreover, very fine and made when the clay is hard. The predominant forms are bottles with stirrup spouts which, in contrast to those of Rocas, have a less thick appearance, and do not have flanges. There are also bowls with slightly divergent straight walls as well as globular pitchers with low and narrow necks. There are not many figurative representations, the decorations being primarily geometrical. One piece is decorated in relief with figures of snails and shells.

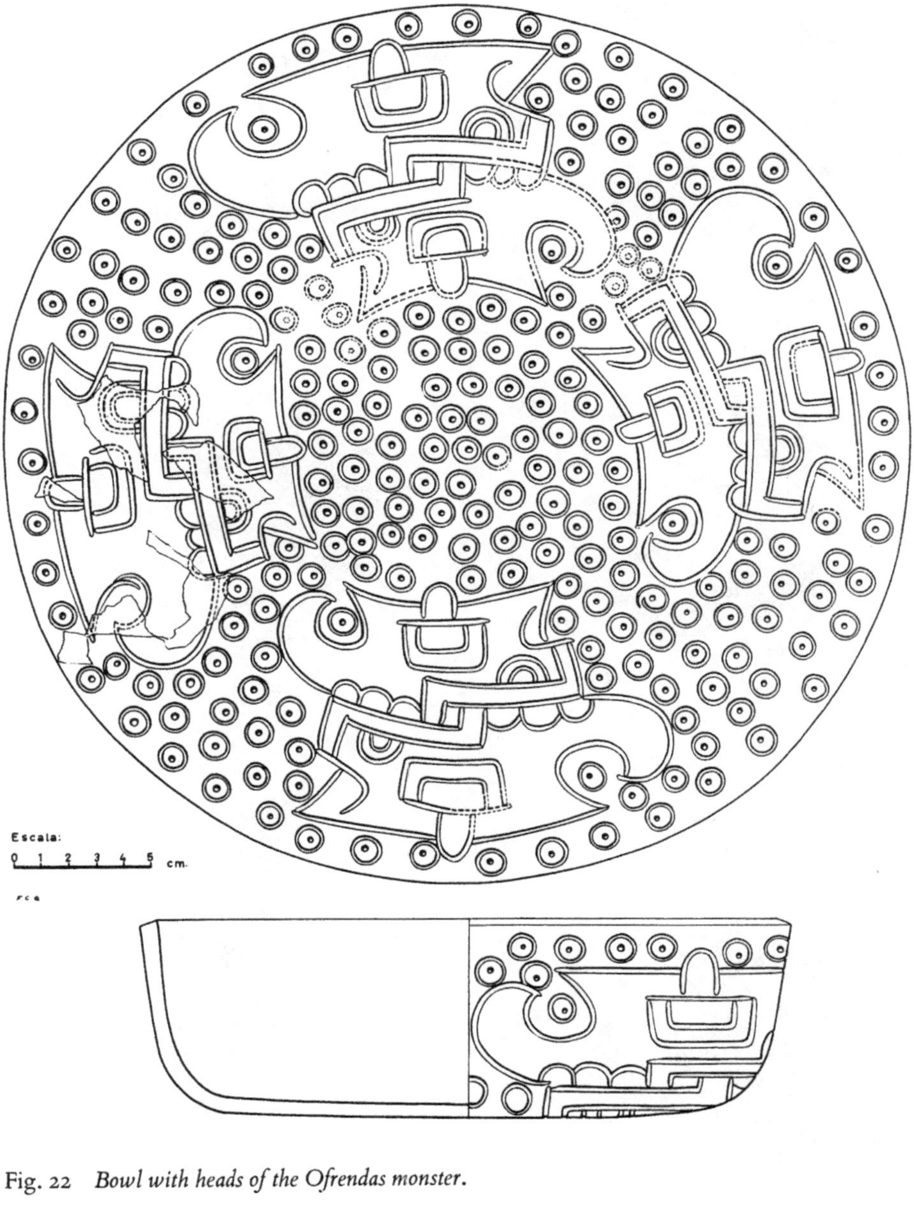

Fig. 22 *Bowl with heads of the Ofrendas monster.*

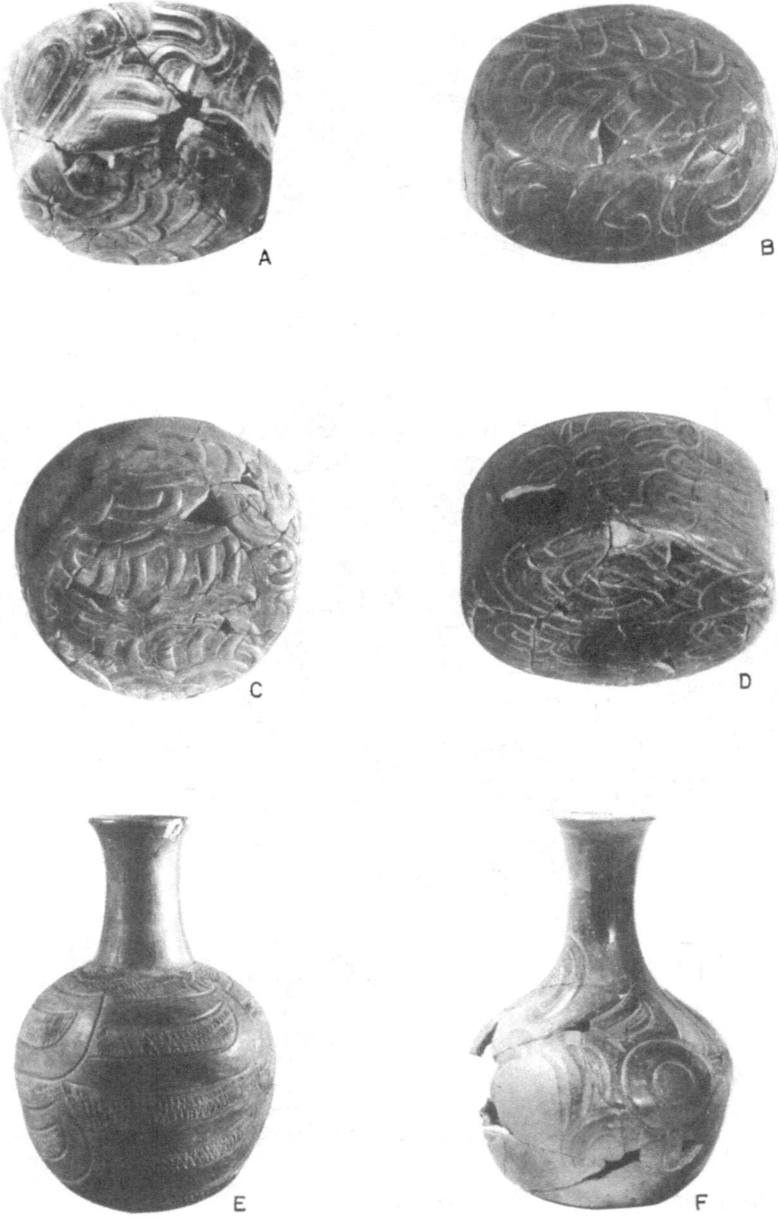

Fig. 23 *Bowls and bottles with representations of the Ofrendas monster.*

Fig. 24 *Wacheqsa stirrup-spout pots, bottles, and bowl.*

Fig. 25 *Mosna pottery.*

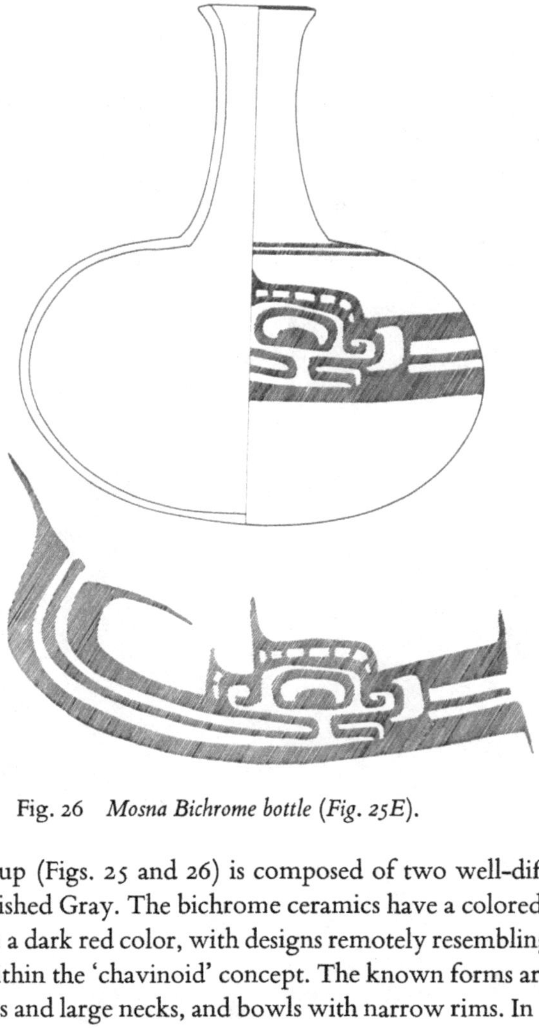

Fig. 26 *Mosna Bichrome bottle (Fig. 25E).*

The Mosna group (Figs. 25 and 26) is composed of two well-differentiated types: Bichrome and Polished Gray. The bichrome ceramics have a colored polished surface, which is painted in a dark red color, with designs remotely resembling those of Chavín and falling well within the 'chavinoid' concept. The known forms are globular bottles with rounded bases and large necks, and bowls with narrow rims. In the gray ware the predominant form is the bottle with the stirrup spout, which has a trapezoidal form, in contrast to Wacheqsa, where the form is rectangular, and to Rocas, where the form is circular.

Apart from the groups that we have been able to identify in Chavín de Huantar thus far, Tello (1960), in his excavations in the same and other places, found fragments of a type which we have tentatively placed between our Rocas and Ofrendas groups, as a transitional stage, in which, moreover, the major portion of Cupisnique type ceramics should be incorporated.

Fig. 27 *Stone objects found at Chavín de Huantar.*

DIFFUSION

There has been much speculation on the origin and expansion of Chavín. Old diffusionist ideas have been reasserted, and recently an attempt has been made to revive theories on the possible Mesoamerican origin of Chavín, theories whose base of support was weakened more than two decades ago. Naturally, all these stem from a limited acquaintance with Chavín. No one, on the other hand, denies that there have been very ancient and permanent contacts between the diverse areas of Nuclear America, and those contacts must have been intensified during the Chavín epoch.

On the other hand, the extent of the influence of Chavín has been slightly exaggerated, having extended, according to some, as far as northwest Argentina. On the basis of our current knowledge, the southern diffusion reached to the region of Ayacucho; its northern limit must be between Piura and Tumbes, with minor influences as far as Azuay, in Ecuador.

The diffusion of Chavín was not accomplished at one time. Thus, the Colinas cemetery in Ancón corresponds to the Ofrendas epoch, while a large part of the ceramics of Chongoyape are of the Rocas type. In Ocucaje (Paracas) it appears that Chavín influenced various epochs. Cupisnique, as we have already said, must correspond in part to the period of transition and in part to Ofrendas.

BIBLIOGRAPHY

AYRES, FRED D.

1961 Rubbings from Chavín de Huántar, Peru. *American Antiquity*, vol. 27, no. 2, pp. 238–245. Salt Lake City.

BENNETT, WENDELL C.

1944 The North Highlands of Peru; Excavations in the Callejón de Huaylas and at Chavín de Huántar. *Anthropological Papers of the American Museum of Natural History*, vol. 39, part 1. New York.

CARRIÓN CACHOT, REBECA

1948 La Cultura Chavín. Dos nuevos colonias: Kuntur Wasi y Ancón. *Revista del Museo Nacional de Antropología y Arqueología*, vol. II, no. 1, pp. 99–172. Lima.

IZUMI, SEIICHI and TOSHIHIKO SONO

1963 Andes 2: Excavations at Kotosh, Peru. Tokyo.

KAUFFMANN, FEDERICO

1963 La Cultura Chavín. Lima.

LARCO HOYLE, RAFAEL

1941 Los Cupisniques. Lima.

MUELLE, JORGE C.

1937 Filogenia de la Estela Raimondi. *Revista del Museo Nacional*, vol. VI, no. 1, pp. 135–150. Lima.

Rowe, John Howland

1962 Chavín Art: An Inquiry into its Form and Meaning. The Museum of Primitive Art, New York.

Tello, Julio C.

1923 Wira-Kocha. Lima.

1929 Antiguo Perú; primera época. Lima.

1934 Origen, desarrollo y correlación de las antiguas culturas peruanas. *Revista de la Universidad Católica del Perú*, año III, tomo II, no. 10, pp. 151–168. Lima.

1943 Discovery of the Chavin Culture in Peru. *American Antiquity*, vol. 9, no. 1, pp. 135–160. Menasha.

1960 Chavín. Cultura matriz de la civilización andina. Primera parte. Publicación Antropológica del Archivo "Julio C. Tello" de la Universidad Nacional Mayor de San Marcos, vol. II. Lima.

Chavín: An Interpretation of Its Spread and Influence

THOMAS C. PATTERSON
YALE UNIVERSITY

THE word Chavín conjures many images, speculations, and questions for the professional archaeologist and laymen alike. Chavín is an incredibly elaborate but puzzling art style with many kinds of complex representations. We may wonder what these representations meant to the ancient Peruvians or what role Chavín played in Andean culture history, and finally, usually in frustration, we may ask ourselves, "What was Chavín really?"

There have been many interpretations of Chavín and its significance. Some represent it as a kind of mother culture influencing all subsequent developments in central Peru (Tello 1943, 1960). Others view it quite differently. Many interpretations involve the idea that Chavín was some sort of religious cult which spread rapidly throughout much of central Peru sometime between about 1300 and 800 B.C. and that, once established, this cult played a prominent role in Andean prehistory for nearly a millennium (e.g., Bennett and Bird 1960: 135–7; Rowe 1962, 1967; Willey 1948).

In the pages that follow, I would like to consider the questions of what Chavín was and the nature of its spread and influence from the perspective of central Peru. When did Chavín influence appear in this area? What patterns of archaeological evidence are associated with it? And how do these patterns of evidence change through time? I then want to view the central Peruvian evidence in light of cultural patterns associated with the spread of Chavín or Chavín influence from other parts of Peru.

In order to do this, it is essential to understand the chronological relationships of what happened. I will use the chronological framework devised by John H. Rowe (1960), which is the one most widely used among specialists in Andean archaeology today. I am concerned mainly with two periods in his framework: the Initial Period and the Early Horizon. The Initial Period began with the appearance of pottery in Ancón about 1750 B.C. and immediately preceded the Early Horizon. The Early Horizon began with the appearance of the resin-painted Paracas pottery in the Ica Valley, an event that presumably occurred about the same time that Chavín influence reached Ica. The available radiocarbon measurements dating the beginning of the Early Horizon conflict with each other so that this event can be dated only roughly between about 1300 and 800 B.C., with about 1000 B.C. being the most reasonable estimate at the present time. The dates for the end of the Early Horizon are also contradictory, but it appears that the period lasted nine hundred years or so. At present, ten chronological subdivisions, numbered 1 through 10, are recognized in the Early Horizon.

For the purpose of this discussion, I am considering central Peru to be the area of the coastal plain and the western slopes of the Andes where my associates and I have been carrying out archaeological research since 1961. This area is roughly L-shaped, extending some 90 kilometers along the coast from Ancón in the north to San Bartolo in the south and more than 100 kilometers inland up the Lurín Valley to the Huarochiri basin in the upper Mala drainage. Central Peru includes not only the sandy beaches, wide alluvial valleys, and quebradas of the coastal plain but also the narrow canyons, gently rolling hills, and ice-covered mountain peaks of the Andes. It contains the desert, stands of *huarango*, and *lomas* vegetation of the coast, as well as the *puna*, barren mountains, and lakes of the highlands. The most striking feature of central Peru is precisely the diversity of its topography and natural environments. It is possible to walk through a half dozen or more different environmental zones in only a few hours. What is more important than the environmental diversity itself is the fact that this variation has played and continues to play a significant role in the daily lives and activities of the central Peruvians.

Cultural diversity accompanies and partly reflects the highly varied environmental conditions of central Peru. The area does not have a uniform culture today, and it is clear from the archaeological and historical record that it did not have one in the past either. Consequently, it is difficult to generalize about the culture history of the area as a whole. What is true about the sequence of events in one part of the area may not be true for developments in another. The easiest way of dealing with this situation is to consider central Peru as being composed of a series of interrelated regions. The nature of the boundaries between these regions, as well as their geographic locations, often changed radically with the passage of time.

We know much more about the culture history of some regions than others, simply because we have worked longer or more intensively in them. This is particularly true of the Ancón-Chillón region, the region around the confluence of the Santa Eulalia and Rimac Rivers, and the Lurín Valley below Sisicaya, where fairly intensive studies have already been carried out. More important than the patterns of archaeological research, however, are the cultural realities represented by the territorial arrangement of this diversity.

The regional cultural patterns indicate that several different social groups have always lived in central Peru at the same time. Each group occupied its own particular territory for long periods of time, and, consequently, there are many small regions in central Peru with virtually uninterrupted histories of human occupation for more than three or four millennia. The territorial arrangement of these groups provided one relatively stable frame of reference by which individuals could relate themselves to other people. What changed in each of these regions were the places where people decided to build their homes, the kinds of settlements they created, and the ways in which they lived. These changes often reflected fluctuations in a second important field of social relations—those between members of different social groups. At times, there was relatively little exchange between members of different groups, and sharp cultural boundaries existed between their territories. At other times, however, there were close ties between different groups, and the locations of the boundaries changed or the boundaries themselves blurred or disappeared altogether.

The simultaneous presence of several social groups in central Peru has other implications also. One of these is how the various groups might interpret and respond to the same situation or problem, such as the appearance of Chavín influence. The archaeological record indicates that they frequently viewed and responded to these situations in quite different ways and that their responses to them often left very different patterns of archaeological evidence.

PATTERNS OF ARCHAEOLOGICAL EVIDENCE IN CENTRAL PERU

The inhabitants of central Peru built three pyramidal structures toward the beginning of the Initial Period. These differ considerably in both size and form from the contemporary domestic architecture and are usually interpreted as some sort of public or ceremonial buildings. The largest of these, the Huaca La Florida, is located in the lower Rimac Valley; the other two, at Mina Perdida in the lower Lurín Valley and at Santa Rosa de Quives in the middle Chillón Valley, are considerably smaller than La Florida but were apparently contemporary with it. All three buildings were abandoned before the appearance of the Colinas and Curayacu pottery styles about the middle of the Initial Period. This does not mark the end of public architecture in central Peru, however, for another large pyramid was built at Garagay midway between the Rimac and Chillón Rivers. A second, much smaller pyramid may also have been built at Malpaso in the middle part of the Lurín Valley.

At the time they used Garagay and Malpaso, the inhabitants of central Peru lived in large fishing villages at Ancón and Curayacu and in small dispersed hamlets in the lower and middle parts of the coastal valleys. Remains of these hamlets have been found in the lower part of the Chillón Valley and in the middle Lurín Valley between Malpaso and Antioquia.

There were at least two distinctive regional ceramic styles in central Peru during the late Initial Period: Curayacu and Colinas (Lanning 1960; Patterson 1968). The Curayacu style has been found at the type site in San Bartolo and in several hamlets in the middle part of the Lurín Valley. The most distinctive feature of the Curayacu style is its red-painted designs which may or may not be outlined with incised lines. The Colinas style, which has been found at Ancón and in the lower Chillón Valley, emphasized zones of punctation outlined with incision, cross-hatching and incision on burnished surfaces, and some surface texturing done with rocker stamping or combing. The surface texturing techniques were innovations in the later phases of the Colinas style. There was some exchange between the inhabitants of the two regions. A few Curayacu-like red-painted vessels have been found in the Colinas levels at Ancón, and a few vessels decorated with zones of punctation occurred at Curayacu; however, these are fairly rare at both sites.

Closely related to the later phases of the Colinas style is the pottery excavated by Gordon R. Willey at the Supe Lighthouse which is located some 125 kilometers north of Ancón (Willey and Corbett 1954). There are features in the Lighthouse style—such as red unslipped surfaces—that never occur in the Colinas assemblages; however, the two styles do share surface texturing techniques—rocker stamping and combed decoration—that distinguish them from Curayacu.

Objects with Chavín or Chavín-influenced designs have been found associated with both the late Colinas and Lighthouse styles; however, these are exceedingly rare. They include a few sherds from different vessels and a small stone pendant decorated with a Chavín design at Ancón and two tapestries with condor representations from Supe (Willey and Corbett 1954: Pls. XXIII and XXIV). No Chavín or Chavín-influenced specimens were found in association with the Curayacu pottery at San Bartolo.

Thus, with respect to Chavín influence during the later part of the Initial Period, we can recognize two very different patterns of archaeological evidence in central Peru. One of these is the pattern at Curayacu, where no Chavín influence occurred at all. The second pattern occurred at both Ancón and the Supe Lighthouse. Here, a few Chavín or Chavín-influenced objects were found associated with the local styles in habitation refuse deposits located in what must have been relatively peripheral fishing villages. In addition to these rare objects, the local ceramic styles of Ancón and Supe incorporated certain surface texturing techniques—rocker stamping and combing—which later became important, integral parts of a widely diffused ceramic style that was associated with the spread of Chavín influence at the beginning of the Early Horizon.

People continued to live at the Ancón and Curayacu fishing villages during the first two epochs of the Early Horizon and exchanged foodstuffs with the farming peoples living in the inland parts of the river valleys. The central Peruvians still used the public buildings at Garagay and Malpaso and may even have built their houses around the pyramid in the middle part of the Lurín Valley. They abandoned some of the small inland hamlets and established others at new locations in the lower and middle parts of the Lurín and presumably in the other valleys as well, even though we have not found them. Only one new site of any consequence may have been established during this period—the small public structure in the lower Lurín Valley which is known as the Huaca Malache. What changed in central Peru during Early Horizon Epochs 1 and 2 was not so much the nature and location of the settlements and architecture, but rather the kinds of pottery that were made and who used them.

In any central Peruvian archaeological site dating to the first two epochs of the Early Horizon, at least three distinctive ceramic styles occur. Edward P. Lanning (1960: 519–20, and personal communication) pointed out that one of these is a widespread style which is also found in contemporary archaeological sites in other areas of Peru. I propose to call this the Yanamanka style in order to distinguish it from other styles that have been called Chavín and incorporate as many local elements as they do Chavín features. Some of these styles date to Early Horizon 1 and 2, while others are earlier or later. Some of the designs in the Yanamanka style are derived from minor elements on the early Chavín stone carvings—feline and bird heads, guilloches, and isolated body parts such as the eccentric eye or bird wings. This ceramic style consists of burnished blackware stirrup-spout bottles, single spout bottles, and bowls. The stirrup-spout bottles have massive, thick spouts and stirrups, flanged lips, and flat bottoms. The single spout bottles also have flanged lips and flat bottoms, as well as gently curving profiles. The standard bowls of the Yanamanka style have thickened flat or beveled rims, occasionally pouring lips, and flat bottoms. Decoration occurs exclusively on the exterior surfaces. In addition to the design motifs already mentioned, there are large concentric circles or targets and relief appliqués. The designs are isolated from each other and floating, and often occur on opposite sides of the vessel. The background may be either polished or textured with rocker stamping, dentate stamping, combing, or small incised dashes. Occasionally, these texturing techniques were used to roughen small parts of the design motifs themselves. It is not yet clear whether the Yanamanka style was made locally in central Peru or was imported from one or a few centers of manufacture, presumably located to the north.

The local ceramic styles of the late Initial Period continued with some modifications into the Early Horizon 1 and 2 levels at both Ancón and Curayacu. The two local styles were still slightly different from each other. The Ancón style was characterized by its use of zoned punctation, and the Early San Bartolo assemblage at Curayacu still contained many vessels with red-painted designs. The boundary separating these two styles seems to have been located near the chain of hills between the Rimac and Lurín Valleys. Sites in the lower and middle Lurín Valley, which date to this period, have pottery assemblages that are virtually indistinguishable from the Early San Bartolo assemblage. Trade continued between the northern and southern regions of the central coast and was perhaps slightly more frequent than it had been in the late Initial Period.

The third set of styles found in the Early Horizon 1 and 2 occupations at Ancón and Curayacu are innovating styles that combine features from both the Yanamanka style and the local pottery traditions. These novel combinations of features were characteristic of neither the Yanamanka nor the local ceramic styles. Vessels in the innovating styles may be as common as those retaining traditional features and certainly more abundant at most sites than Yanamanka pottery. The innovating styles must have had considerable prestige, for the features of these styles rather than those of the local traditions or Yanamanka seem to predominate in the later pottery styles of central Peru.

Some pottery manufactured outside of central Peru also occurs in the Early Horizon 1 and 2 assemblages of Ancón and Curayacu. Trade pieces are not particularly common at either site but may be slightly more abundant at Curayacu than at Ancón. Although these have not been analyzed in detail, a considerable number of them either came from the south coast of Peru or incorporated design features that were characteristic of this area.

The patterns of archaeological evidence for Chavín influence in central Peru during Early Horizon 1 and 2 are both similar and different from those that prevailed during the later part of the Initial Period. First, Yanamanka pottery with its Chavín-influenced designs is not limited just to burials, special offering pits, or deposits located near public buildings. It is equally common in everyday habitation refuse deposits at peripheral fishing villages like Ancón or Curayacu and presumably in the hamlets and villages located in the inland parts of the coastal river valleys. In this respect, the pattern resembles that of the Initial Period; however, the evidence of Chavín influence is many times more abundant than it had been previously. It probably should be pointed out that the abundance of Yanamanka pottery in habitation refuse deposits contrasts markedly with the distribution of the prestige styles in either the Middle Horizon or the Late Horizon. Second, the Yanamanka style and the local innovating style appear suddenly as a complex in the Early San Bartolo occupation at Curayacu. This contrasts with the pattern that occurred at Ancón, where the appearance of the Yanamanka and local innovating styles seems much less sudden, because some of the features of both were already present in the late Initial Period pottery of the region. Third, the tremendous impact that Chavín influence had on the artisans of central

Peru is perhaps the most important feature of Early Horizon 1 and 2. By the end of the period, the local pottery styles were based mainly on the Yanamanka and innovating styles, and many of the traditional features either disappeared or became exceedingly rare.

Epochs 3 and 4 of the Early Horizon seem to be a time when relatively rapid and complex social changes were taking place in central Peru. It is difficult to deal with this period, partly because of its complexity and partly because the relative chronology has not been worked out in sufficient detail. Undoubtedly, some of the difficulties will resolve themselves once a more detailed chronology has been established, and a clearer picture of what happened will emerge.

Virtually every conceivable change in settlement patterns that could have taken place occurred during Early Horizon 3 and 4. Several small hamlets, as well as the Huaca Malache in the lower Lurín Valley, were abandoned about the beginning of the period. Other sites—such as Ancón, Curayacu, Malpaso, and probably Garagay—continued to be occupied throughout the period. A new kind of settlement appeared at the beginning of Early Horizon 4 in the middle Rimac Valley, replacing the previous pattern of dispersed houses along the sides of the hills overlooking the valley floor. It consisted of several hundred adjacent and/or adjoining rooms that were laid out in a more or less rectangular pattern; associated with this room complex were two semisubterranean circular courtyards. Sunken circular courtyards may also have been built during Early Horizon 4 at Malpaso in the middle Lurín Valley and at another site in the middle part of the Chillón Valley (José Casafranca and Gary S. Vescelius, personal communication). And finally, several sites—e.g., Curayacu and the site in the middle Rimac—were abandoned at the end of the period.

A series of regionally distinct pottery styles existed in central Peru during this period. One was centered around Ancón and presumably the lower parts of the Chillón and Rimac Valleys. Another occurred in the south coastal region of central Peru around the Curayacu site. A third set of styles was found in the middle parts of the Lurín and Rimac Valleys. All of the central Peruvian styles at this time shared many features but can be distinguished from each other by their selection of different features for emphasis. For example, the pottery of the middle elevations in the valleys was lighter in color than that found in either of the coastal regions. Designs derived from minor elements of the Chavín C and D stone sculptural styles occurred in each of the regional ceramic assemblages; however, the Chavín elements seem to have been borrowed individually and placed in new contexts on vessels—for example, the eagle wings on plate and bowl interiors in the Ancón assemblages. There is nothing in any of the central Peruvian pottery assemblages of this period that resembles the Yanamanka style of earlier times.

Pieces of foreign manufacture continued to appear in central Peru during this period and may even have been more abundant than in the preceding one, particularly in the south coastal region around Curayacu. The Late San Bartolo levels contained Paracas trade sherds from Ica, the Chincha area, fragments of Topará pottery that was presumably from Cañete, and pieces of a purple-on-orange style, the origins of which are unknown but presumably in the central highlands (Lanning, personal communication).

Three major patterns can be discerned in central Peru during this period. The most apparent is cultural or regional diversification. A new social group emerged to establish itself in the middle parts of the Lurín and Rimac Valleys; the archaeological patterns that distinguish this region from the coastal ones include lighter-colored pottery, the presence of semi-subterranean circular courtyards, and nucleated villages. The second pattern that emerged was one of increased communication and contact between the peoples of the south coastal region of central Peru and those who lived in the area from Cañete to Ica. Finally, Chavín influence was still apparent in both the pottery and architecture, but it appeared more as a series of isolated traits than as a complex of features. It may also have been more intense at the middle elevations than on the coast and more intense in the northern coastal region than in the southern one.

It is also difficult to deal with the later part of the Early Horizon in central Peru. This is not because the data are scarce but rather because no one has systematically analyzed them yet. The period is much longer than those already discussed, and, consequently, the patterns that emerge are not as specific as those already mentioned. This situation will undoubtedly be remedied once the available materials have been studied in more detail.

People continued to live at Ancón throughout the period and probably still used the public buildings at Malpaso and Garagay, at least during the early part of it—perhaps Early Horizon 5 and 6. At the same time, they built two complexes of public buildings on opposite sides of the lower Lurín Valley; these buildings were subsequently abandoned, well before the end of the Early Horizon. Toward the end of the period—perhaps Early Horizon 8 or 9—a new kind of settlement appeared in central Peru. These were hilltop villages that were occasionally fortified. They were located in the lower Chillón Valley and in the middle parts of the Rimac and Lurín Valleys. About this time, the inhabitants also abandoned many of the small dispersed hamlets that previously existed in these regions.

The regionally distinct ceramic styles of the preceding period continued until about the beginning of Early Horizon 7. One was found at Ancón and presumably in the lower Chillón Valley as well. Another occurred in the lower Lurín Valley in the south coastal region of central Peru. The third style was still centered in the middle of the

Lurín Valley. During the last three epochs of the Early Horizon, we can distinguish four regional styles in central Peru: Ancón, the lower Chillón Valley and presumably the Rimac as well, the lower Lurín Valley, and the middle parts of the Lurín and Rimac Valleys.

None of the regional styles dating to Early Horizon 5 and 6 appear to contain Chavín design elements, although all of them still had the surface texturing techniques that were formerly associated with Chavín influence. If Chavín designs did occur, then they must have been exceedingly rare. It is clear that none of the ceramic styles after Early Horizon 7 contained any Chavín design elements at all. These styles either lacked decoration altogether or made minimal use of incision and painting.

No vessels of foreign manufacture have yet been recognized in any of the assemblages dating between Epochs 5 and 8 of the Early Horizon. Two trade pieces—one from Ancón and the other from the lower Rimac Valley—were made on the south coast of Peru and date to the end of the Early Horizon.

Several major patterns can be recognized during this period. The first is that there was a considerable reduction in the amount of Chavín influence that can be seen in the pottery. This influence disappeared altogether toward the end of the period. The second pattern is a continuation of the trend toward regional or cultural diversification that began in Early Horizon 3 and 4. The third pattern is one of increasing isolation from other areas of Peru; there is no evidence of foreign contacts except at the end of the Early Horizon and the beginning of the Early Intermediate Period. The fourth pattern is one of increased warfare or raiding during the later part of the Early Horizon. It is not yet clear whether the groups involved were exclusively from central Peru or whether groups from other areas were also involved.

PATTERNS OF ARCHAEOLOGICAL EVIDENCE IN OTHER AREAS OF PERU

In other areas, we can recognize two distinct patterns of archaeological evidence with respect to the presence of Chavín or Chavín influence during the Initial Period. They are the same ones that emerge from the central Peruvian materials. The first is that there is no evidence of Chavín-influenced trade pieces or of Chavín influence in the local pottery styles. This pattern occurs in the late Initial Period pottery of the Paracas-Ica area on the south coast and of the Piura-Chira area on the far north coast (Lanning 1960).

The second pattern is one where certain features that were subsequently incorporated into the Yanamanka style occurred in late Initial Period ceramic assemblages. This pattern is represented by the Kotosh Kotosh assemblage of the Huánuco area, the Late Toril assemblage of the Callejón de Huaylas, and the Middle Guañape assemblage of the Virú Valley (Strong and Evans 1952: 23–46, 253–9, 277–94; Izumi and Sono 1963; Vescelius, personal communication). The Yanamanka features found in these styles are mainly surface texturing techniques, such as plain rocker stamping or combed decoration; however, stirrup-spout bottle fragments also occurred in the Kotosh Kotosh levels. As far as I know, nothing resembling the Supe textiles or the pottery and pendant from Ancón have been found in any of the areas in north central Peru in a demonstrable late Initial Period context.

There is an important feature of the distribution of Yanamanka design elements and Chavín-influenced objects during the late Initial Period that should be pointed out. Their distribution correlates exactly with the known distribution of public buildings during the Initial Period (Lanning 1967: 90–5). These include Garagay, Culebras 1 in the Culebras Valley, Las Haldas near Casma, Huaricanga in the middle Fortaleza Valley, Huaricoto in the Callejón de Huaylas, the Temple of the Llamas in the lower Virú Valley, and Kotosh.

Chavín influence spread rapidly and widely during Early Horizon 1, and we can recognize four ways in which it was accepted in different areas. The first pattern of acceptance occurs in regions like Curayacu where the Yanamanka style appears suddenly, and a local innovating style develops almost immediately. The second pattern of acceptance occurs in areas where some Yanamanka design features were already present in the local pottery traditions of the late Initial Period—Huánuco, Virú-Chicama, and the Callejón de Huaylas. In these areas, the Yanamanka style also appears suddenly, but it seems much less intrusive here than it does where the local pottery styles did not include Yanamanka surface texturing techniques or vessel shapes. Innovating styles develop immediately in these areas, incorporating Yanamanka features as well as those of the local traditions. It is these innovating styles that give each Early Horizon 1 and 2 pottery assemblage its own distinctive appearance. For example, stamped design elements are a prominent feature in the Kotosh Chavín assemblage, but they occur only on trade pieces in the central coastal assemblages where the use of Yanamanka techniques in local geometric designs is the characteristic feature of the local styles.

No Yanamanka pottery vessels have ever been reported from areas where the other two patterns of acceptance occur. One of these patterns is represented by the Paracas styles of the south coast of Peru (Menzel, Rowe, and Dawson 1964). The Paracas potters copied Chavín and Yanamanka designs and were profoundly influenced by the two styles. At the same time, however, they continued to maintain local specialities, such as double spout bottles, which gave their style its highly distinctive character. The other pattern of acceptance is represented by the Paita and Pechiche styles of the far north coast of Peru (Lanning 1963; Izumi and Terada 1966). In these areas, Yanamanka and Chavín design elements were occasionally borrowed by the local potters, and they appear on a few vessels in each of the styles; however, Yanamanka and Chavín influence never became predominant in either of the two local styles.

Associated with the spread of Chavín influence during the Early Horizon was the construction and/or remodeling of large public buildings in north central Peru. Unfortunately, few of these buildings have been studied in detail; however, examinations of their pottery assemblages and Rowe's analysis of the Chavín designs found at several of them show clearly that these structures were not all contemporary with each other (Rowe 1962, 1967). At least two of the buildings—Garagay and Huaricoto—were begun in the Initial Period, judging by the pottery associated with their early building stages. The pottery assemblages illustrated from Pallca in the Casma Valley (Tello 1943: Pl. xv; 1956: Figs. 7–20) contain a number of Yanamanka fragments which suggest that the site dates at least in part to Epochs 1 and 2 of the Early Horizon. The adobe murals at Cerro Blanco in the Nepeña Valley have been assigned to Phase C of the Chavín style, which suggests that this construction phase probably dates to Early Horizon 3 (Rowe 1967: 76). The feline at Punkuri in Nepeña has a turned-up mouth which resembles those of Chavín Phase D; this suggests that Punkuri may belong to Early Horizon 4 (Larco Hoyle 1938, vol. 1: 32–8; 1941: Fig. 7). A lintel at La Copa near Cajamarca belongs to Chavín Phase EF which is probably no earlier than Early Horizon 4 and may even be later (Rowe 1967: 76). Other sites constructed at least in part during the Early Horizon are Pacopampa and Mojeque, though evidence for dating them more specifically is lacking at the present time.

Each of the public buildings in north central Peru that was used during the Early Horizon has its own distinctive architecture, even though they share a number of distinctive features with each other. One architectural innovation that appears at a number of the sites is a sunken courtyard. The courtyard built at Chavín de Huantar at the time the Black and White Portal was set in place is rectangular. Judging by the fact that the stone sculpture of the Black-and-White Portal belongs to Phase D of the Chavín style, the construction of the courtyard probably took place in Early Horizon 4 (Rowe 1967: 74–7; Menzel, Rowe, and Dawson 1964: 258). All of the other sunken courtyards that have been reported are circular and considerably smaller than the one at Chavín itself. Gary S. Vescelius (personal communication) has reported that two lateral wings and a circular, semi-subterranean court were built at Huaricoto at the beginning of the Capilla 3 phase which he dates to Early Horizon 4. These courtyards are therefore approximately contemporary with the ones that were built at sites in the middle parts of the Rimac and Lurín Valleys in central Peru.

The detailed analysis of Paracas pottery by Menzel, Rowe, and Dawson (1964: 257–62) showed that the nature and intensity of Chavín influence varied considerably in the development of this south coast style. Close resemblances existed between the two styles in Early Horizon 1 and 2 and again in Early Horizon 4 and 5, when a number of new Chavín features made their appearance on the south coast. Paracas and Chavín also shared general stylistic trends from Early Horizon 1 to 8. No such detailed analyses have been made for other styles dating to the Early Horizon; however, the studies that are available suggest that the same pattern of variation in intensity and changes in the kinds of Chavín features that are incorporated into the local styles holds in other areas as well.

Another important question concerning Chavín influence is when it disappeared in different areas. The analysis of the Paracas styles shows that Chavín features were incorporated into the local traditions from Early Horizon 1 to 8 and that no new Chavín features were incorporated after that time (Menzel, Rowe, and Dawson 1964: 257–62). Vescelius (personal communication) has pointed out that Chavín-influenced pottery disappeared in the Callejón de Huaylas at the end of the Capilla style which occurred in Early Horizon 6; however, he sees no relationships between Chavín Phase EF and the subsequent Huaraz ware which appears in the sequence during Epoch 7 of the Early Horizon and disappears shortly after the beginning of the Early Intermediate Period. At Kotosh, obvious Chavín-influenced design features are limited exclusively to the Kotosh Chavín assemblage, which probably dates exclusively to the first four epochs of the Early Horizon; no obvious Chavín-influenced designs can be recognized in the Sajara-patac style which probably began about Early Horizon 5 and persisted into the early part of the Early Intermediate Period (Izumi and Sono 1963; Vescelius, personal communication). Chavín-influenced designs occur throughout the Cupisnique A and B styles on the north coast; Yanamanka surface texturing techniques continue into the first phase of the Cupisnique C substyle which probably dates to about Early Horizon 6 (Rowe 1958). Subsequently, Chavín-influenced designs appear to be absent or very rare on Cupisnique pottery; however, they reappear as archaisms on a number of Moche III pieces dating to the middle of the Early Intermediate Period.

The pattern that emerges from this is that Chavín influence as represented in local pottery styles disappears at different times in the various areas. It disappears first in the Huánuco area and then in central Peru and perhaps on the north coast. It persists for the longest period of time in the Callejón de Huaylas. It is not clear, however, whether this pattern merely reflects changes in taste where representational art is replaced by abstract geometric designs or whether it in fact actually represents the disappearance of Chavín influence in each of these areas.

Another widespread pattern at the end of the Early Horizon—perhaps Epochs 8 and 9—is the construction of hilltop villages, many of which are fortified in one way or another. One of these is Tajahuana in the Ica Valley which was occupied exclusively during Early Horizon 9. Other examples of fortified hilltop sites dating roughly to this period are Chanquillo in the Casma Valley and a series of sites in the middle part of the Santa Valley (Vescelius, personal communication; Collier 1962: 413). The reason for the construction of fortified hilltop settlements over such a vast area at approximately the same time is not immediately apparent. Possibly it is associated in some way with the spread of Paracas and Topará influence northward along the coast near the end of the Early Horizon.

CHAVÍN: AN INTERPRETATION

In the preceding pages, I have presented and discussed a considerable amount of evidence relating to Chavín influence and its spread throughout much of central Peru during the first millennium B.C., but I have still not suggested an answer to the question of what Chavín was.

Many archaeologists and laymen alike hold the view that Chavín was some kind of religious cult. This view is based on several lines of evidence. The first of these consists of the nature of the representations on Chavín stone sculpture and the contexts in which some of the representations occur at Chavín de Huantar. Rowe (1967) has set forth the most detailed and convincing presentation of this view. To summarize his argument, there are several representations in the Chavín style that have elaborate kennings and do not represent natural forms. One of these is the Great Image, or Smiling God, which is located in a dark passageway in the middle of the oldest part of the temple at Chavín. A later representation of the Smiling God occurs on a small flat sculpture set in the wall of a patio in front of the old south wing. The latter, he argues, provided a representation of the Smiling God for those worshipers who were not admitted to the inner part of the shrine. A second figure of mythological importance, identified as the Staff God, occurs on the Raimondi Stele and on a gold plaque in the Rafael Larco Herrera Museum. Rowe argues by analogy that the Raimondi Stele was probably also set in an outside wall, that it is probably a representation of the deity worshiped in the old south wing, and that it was intended to be seen by those who could not enter this part of the building. On the gold plaque, the Staff God is accompanied by two smaller attendant figures that have the same combination of human and bird attributes as those on the columns of the Black and White Portal in front of the first addition to the old south wing.

Another line of evidence that is frequently cited in support of the idea that Chavín was a religious cult consists of the imposing public buildings that were built in other areas of Peru during the Early Horizon and decorated with Chavín motifs in their stone sculpture or adobe reliefs.

I find the argument that a religious cult is represented by the patterns of archaeological evidence to be a convincing one and accept it as the most reasonable interpretation of these data at the present time. However, this does not tell us when the cult began, where it began, how it spread, or even what it was like. These are questions that I would now like to deal with.

The religious cult represented at Chavín de Huantar was already widespread in central and north-central Peru during the later part of the Initial Period, before the temple at Chavín de Huantar was built about the beginning of the Early Horizon. The people of Ancón and Supe were certainly aware of this cult, and possibly its system of beliefs as well, for a few objects decorated with Chavín designs have been found at both sites. The cult was probably also known from Huánuco to the Callejón de Huaylas in the highlands and from the Rimac Valley to Chicama on the coast, where, during the late Initial Period, design elements and techniques that were later incorporated into the Yanamanka style were already being used in the pottery styles of these areas.

In my readings about the expansion of the Christian church during the first three centuries I noticed that there were a number of parallels in the patterns of archaeological evidence associated with its spread and those related to the spread of Chavín in the late Initial Period. We would be hard-pressed to prove that a religious cult was spreading throughout the Mediterranean world and part of the Near East during the first two centuries if we had to rely solely on archaeological evidence and did not have access to written records. There were only a few truly distinctive pieces of early Christian art during this period; more common, however, were objects done in one of many local styles, to which the Christians attached special significance. These objects shared themes and features of design or composition regardless of what local style they were executed in.

An important question that we should ask is what conditions might have facilitated the spread of the Chavín cult during the late Initial Period. Again, a comparison with the conditions related to the spread of early Christianity provides several useful lines of inference. Early Christianity was an urban religion which spread from Palestine along ancient, pre-Roman trade routes to urban centers around the Mediterranean and in the Near East. Its spread during the first two centuries did not correspond exactly with the boundaries of the Roman Empire. What its spread did reflect, however, was the distribution of urban centers with synagogues and large Greek-speaking communities. The synagogues formed an already established network for carrying the new religion from one urban center to another. Later, the Christian communities themselves took over this function and sent missionaries to preach their message to the uninitiated in other urban areas. Greek was the language used to communicate the new doctrine at first, and then later Latin was used, particularly in the Western part of the Empire. Three other factors also facilitated the spread of Christianity during the first two or three centuries. One was the relatively peaceful conditions that existed as a result of the Pax Romana. Another was the religious tolerance of the Romans, who asked no more than that the state deities be worshiped at the appropriate times. The third was the simultaneous spread of other religions which shared features with Christianity but competed with it at first (Harnack 1961: 19–33). During the late Initial Period, the Chavín cult was known precisely in those areas where public architecture and occasionally urban centers already existed. There is no evidence as yet that the cult was known outside of central and north-central Peru and little indication that warfare or unsettled political conditions existed in Peru.

The variation in ceramic styles and architectural patterns in the late Initial Period, both before and after Chavín influence can be discerned, may also reflect a situation resembling another facet of the early Christian church. Neither the Judaism out of which Christianity emerged nor early Christianity itself had single unified doctrines. A missionary sent from Antioch, for example, preached the religion in a different way than one from the Christian communities in Rome or Jerusalem. There were probably also differences in the way he talked about Christianity in the towns of northern or central Europe and in the urban centers of Syria. The doctrinal disputes and heresies of the first three centuries, which had largely regional bases, also indicate that the interpretations and practice of Christianity varied somewhat from one area to another.

Chavín probably became a pan-Peruvian religion in Early Horizon 1, and its sphere of influence increased greatly at this time as peoples living outside of the old Initial Period core area accepted some or all of the religious teachings of the cult. The spread of the religion was not associated with military conquest; the peoples outside of the core area accepted it either through a desire to imitate or to be in close contact with the adherents of the faith. This pattern also has analogies with the spread of Christianity after it became a state religion in the fourth century. Christianity spread outside of the Empire during this period, not so much by military conquest on the part of the Romans, but rather by its acceptance by peoples who were impressed with the grandeur of Rome or who wanted to establish trade or other sorts of relations with the state. The archaeological record in these areas shows a variety of patterns representing the way in which Christianity was accepted. A similar variety of patterns can be recognized in the Peruvian data. The Chavín cult was apparently accepted completely and quickly by the inhabitants of the south coastal region of central Peru, where the

Yanamanka style appears suddenly in deposits of habitation refuse. The new religion was accepted quickly by the inhabitants of the south coast of Peru but perhaps less completely than by their neighbors to the north. The designs of the Yanamanka style were copied by the local artisans but not always so faithfully as in other regions; the art, and possibly the religion as well, maintained a highly distinctive local character in the Ica-Cañete area. Possibly the area was missionized by peoples from the central highlands of Peru, where resin-painted pottery was being used during the late Initial Period. The Chavín religion was probably not accepted at all by the inhabitants of the far north coast, who occasionally borrowed designs from its art style but never in any systematic way.

The increasing regionalization of Peruvian cultures during Early Horizon 3 and 4 suggests that the Chavín cult was breaking up into a series of local cults, each of which may have emphasized different aspects of the ancient religion but still maintained contacts with the principal centers. There was also substantial construction activity at Chavín de Huantar itself during this period that seems to be associated with the increasing importance of the Staff God who was housed in the new addition to the old south wing. This building activity is also reflected in the construction of sunken circular courtyards at Huaricoto in the Callejón de Huaylas, at sites in the middle parts of the Lurín and Rimac Valleys, and perhaps at Las Haldas south of the Casma Valley (Rosa Fung, personal communication). This suggests that the Staff God may have replaced earlier cult figures as the most important Chavín deity in these areas, as well as on the south coast where textiles bearing his representation have been found. Older cult figures—such as the one represented by the cayman—may have remained important at some sites in the north highlands. At other sites, new cult figures—such as the unique representation at La Copa—may have gained regional importance. In addition, many regionally important cult centers were built in Early Horizon 4 and 5 on the central coast and between the Huarmey and Casma Valleys on the north central coast (Thompson 1962).

This process of regionalization continued throughout the remainder of the Early Horizon, and the regional cults may have begun to replace Chavín in importance. Chavín influence persisted for periods of greater or lesser duration in the different areas of Peru. Huánuco and central Peru apparently severed their ties with the Chavín cult shortly after the Staff God attained importance, judging by the lack of Chavín-influenced designs in the local art styles of these areas after Early Horizon 5. Other areas—such as Cajamarca, the north coast, and Ica-Paracas—continued to maintain contacts with the principal Chavín centers until Early Horizon 7 or 8, when they too ceased to have close affinities with these centers. The Callejón de Huaylas continued to display ties with the centers until the end of the Early Horizon. Judging by the kinds of designs that were incorporated into the local art styles, the kind of Chavín influence that was accepted in each of these areas was probably different.

Toward the end of the Early Horizon, perhaps Epochs 8 to 10, there was a marked increase in warfare, judging by the large number of fortified hilltop sites that were built and occupied during this time. This pattern of warfare may represent raiding between groups of people who were attempting to gain control over the same set of resources, whether they be natural or human. We know relatively little about the cultural relationships that existed during this period, except on the south coast of Peru. Here the center of the Paracas culture was first in the Ica Valley and then in Nasca. By Early Horizon 8, there were close contacts between the south coast and the Huanta area of the south central highlands, where a local art style that is closely related to Paracas has been found. The Paracas sphere of influence eventually spread into the south highlands, where representations of Paracas mythical beings dating to Early Horizon 9 and 10 have been found on local pottery as far south as Tiahuanaco. At the same time, the peoples of the Cañete, Chincha, and Pisco Valleys were beginning to exert considerable influence on the local art styles of the Ica Valley and the central Peruvian coast, as far north as Lomas Lachay.

It is well known that Chavín art was revived at various times after the end of the Early Horizon. There are two periods in particular when these revivals occurred. The first took place on the north Peruvian coast towards the end of the Early Intermediate Period; it consists of the Moche III imitations of Cupisnique pottery. The second period of revival occurred during the Middle Horizon. In addition to the imitation Chavín pottery that has been found in Middle Horizon 1B contexts on the central and north coasts of Peru, the deities represented in the art of both Huari and Tiahuanaco have the same pose as the Staff God and are often flanked by attendant figures, some of which combine bird and human attributes, like those on the columns of the Black-and-White Portal at Chavín de Huantar or on the gold plaque that has already been mentioned. Rowe (1967: 87) suggested that the poses of the Huari and Tiahuanaco deities represent the transmission of certain conventions of religious art from Chavín to the Middle Horizon cultures. An alternative to Rowe's suggestion is that something more than conventions of religious art was passed down from Chavín to the Middle Horizon cultures and that the Huari and Tiahuanaco deities with the Staff God poses are later representations of this cult figure. This suggestion presupposes some kind of direct transmission from Chavín to the Middle Horizon cultures. Since these are separated in time from each other by six or seven centuries, it is necessary to find antecedents for the Huari and Tiahuanaco deities which date to the Early Intermediate Period and which are derived from the Chavín figure. The Pucara style of the south highlands, which belongs to the early part of the Early Intermediate Period, conceivably represents one intermediary step in the transmission; however, as yet there are no known antecedents for the Staff God which date to the later part of the Early Intermediate Period and immediately precede the appearance of these representations in Middle Horizon art.

The meager amount of information that is available for the Early Intermediate Period occupations in vast areas of the highlands neither supports nor refutes the argument that the cult of the Staff God continued from Chavín to Huari and Tiahuanaco. Assuming that there was transmission of more than conventions of religious art, the question I would pose is, what elements of Huari or Tiahuanaco religion could have occurred in the Chavín cult? Oracles may be one such element. There are two indications of the presence of oracles in the Huari religion. One consists of a stone statue found in the Ayacucho area which represents a human figure. The back of the statue has a large depression which could conceal a full-grown man, and a hollowed tube extends from the mouth to the back of the statue. The other consists of the Temple of Pachacamac, located on the coast, which housed a famous oracle during the Inca Period. The structure in which the oracle was located was built in Middle Horizon 2B, a period of heavy Huari influence on the central coast. An early chronicler described the Inca Period oracle as a piece of wood, set in a dark room on top of the mound. A carved piece of wood, about two meters tall, was found on top of the Temple of Pachacamac in the late 1930's and is now on display in the Pachacamac Museum; the designs on the wood sculpture date to Middle Horizon 2B. The construction date of the Temple of Pachacamac and the Middle Horizon 2B wood carving suggest that oracles had a long history at Pachacamac (Patterson 1966). The evidence for oracles at Chavín de Huantar consists of the arrangement of rooms in the oldest building stage where the Great Image, or Smiling God, is located. Immediately above the chamber of the Great Image is another room or passage. There is a small opening connecting the two rooms near the top of the Great Image. It is conceivable that voices coming from the upper room would be heard below.

I have dealt primarily with the spread of Chavín influence from its beginning in the late Initial Period to its decline towards the middle and later parts of the Early Horizon. The data, conclusions, and speculations presented here should not be taken as the final words about the spread and nature of Chavín influence or about the nature of the Chavín cult itself. Instead, they should be viewed as first statements that will be modified as new evidence becomes available and that raise new questions about the evidence already at hand. They focus attention on such questions as the kinds of relationships existing between the principal Chavín cult centers and the outlying areas or why peoples decide to accept new religions and to incorporate the symbolism into their own artistic traditions.

ACKNOWLEDGMENTS This paper could not have been written without the assistance and cooperation of many individuals. I particularly want to thank Hernan Amat, Rosa Fung, Michael Harner, Edward P. Lanning, John H. Rowe, Janet Siskind, Harry G. Scheele, and Gary S. Vescelius for discussing their unpublished research with me. The analogy between the spread of early Christianity and Chavín which underlies much of what is said in this paper has profited considerably from the comments of Edward P. Lanning and Michael D. Coe. Support for much of the research on which this paper is based has been provided by the National Science Foundation, Yale University, and Mrs. Gertrude M. Connor of New York, all of whom I wish to thank for their assistance.

BIBLIOGRAPHY

BENNETT, WENDELL C. and JUNIUS B. BIRD

1960 Andean Culture History. (Second and revised edition.) American Museum of Natural History, Handbook Series, no. 15. New York.

COLLIER, DONALD

1962 Archaeological Investigations in the Casma Valley, Peru. Akten des 34. Internationalen Amerikanistenkongresses, pp. 411–417. Horn-Vienna.

HARNACK, ADOLF VON

1961 The Mission and Expansion of Christianity in the First Three Centuries. (James Moffatt, trans. and ed.) New York.

IZUMI, SEIICHI and TOSHIHKO SONO

1963 Andes 2. Excavations at Kotosh, Peru, 1960. Tokyo.

IZUMI, SEIICHI and KAZUO TERADA

1966 Andes 3. Excavations at Pechiche and Garbanzal, Tumbes Valley, Peru, 1960. Tokyo.

LANNING, EDWARD P.

1963 A Ceramic Sequence for the Piura and Chira coast, North Peru. *University of California Publications in American Archaeology and Ethnology*, vol. 46, no. 2, pp. 135–184. Berkeley and Los Angeles.

1967 Peru Before the Incas. Englewood Cliffs, New Jersey.

n.d. Chronological and Cultural Relationships of Early Pottery Styles in Ancient Peru. (Unpublished Ph.D. dissertation, 1960.) University of California, Berkeley.

LARCO HOYLE, RAFAEL

1938–39 Los Mochicas. 2 vols. Lima.

1941 Los Cupisniques. Lima.

MENZEL, DOROTHY, JOHN H. ROWE, and LAWRENCE E. DAWSON

1964 The Paracas Pottery of Ica: A Study in Style and Time. *University of California Publications in American Archaeology and Ethnology*, vol. 50. Berkeley and Los Angeles.

PARKE, HERBERT W.

1967 Greek Oracles. London.

PATTERSON, THOMAS C.

1968 Current Research. *American Antiquity*, vol. 33, no. 3, pp. 422–424. Salt Lake City.

n.d. The Oracle and the Inca: The Role of Pachacamac in Andean Culture History. (Paper presented at the Annual Meeting of the Society for American Archaeology, Reno, Nevada, 1966.)

ROWE, JOHN HOWLAND

1960 Cultural Unity and Diversification in Peruvian Archaeology. *In* Men and Cultures; Selected Papers of the Fifth International Congress of Anthropological and Ethnological Sciences, pp. 627–631. University of Pennsylvania Press, Philadelphia.

1962 Chavín Art: An Inquiry into its Form and Meaning. The Museum of Primitive Art, New York.

1967 Form and Meaning in Chavin Art. *In* Peruvian Archaeology; Selected Readings (John H. Rowe and Dorothy Menzel, eds.), pp. 72–103. Palo Alto.

n.d. Seriation of Cupisnique Stirrup Spouts. (Dittoed manuscript, 5 pp.) Berkeley.

STRONG, WILLIAM D. and CLIFFORD EVANS, JR.

1952 Cultural Stratigraphy in the Virú Valley, Northern Peru. *Columbia Studies in Archeology and Ethnology*, vol. IV. New York.

TELLO, JULIO C.

1943 Discovery of the Chavín Culture in Peru. *American Antiquity*, vol. 9, no. 1, pp. 135–160. Menasha.

1956 Arqueología del Valle de Casma. Culturas: Chavín, Santa o Huaylas Yunga u Sub-Chimú. Publicación Antropológica del Archivo "Julio C. Tello" de la Universidad Nacional Mayor de San Marcos, vol. I. Lima.

1960 Chavín. Cultura matriz de la civilización andina. Primera parte. Publicación Antropológica del Archivo "Julio C. Tello" de la Universidad Nacional Mayor de San Marcos, vol. II. Lima.

THOMPSON, DONALD E.

1962 The Problem of Dating Certain Stone-Faced, Stepped Pyramids on the North Coast of Peru. *Southwestern Journal of Anthropology*, vol. 18, no. 4, pp. 291–301. Albuquerque.

WILLEY, GORDON R.

1948 Functional Analysis of "Horizon Styles" in Peruvian Archaeology. *In* A Reappraisal of Peruvian Archaeology (Wendell C. Bennett, ed.), *Memoirs of the Society for American Archaeology*, no. 4, pp. 8–15. Menasha.

WILLEY, GORDON R. and JOHN M. CORBETT

1954 Early Ancon and Early Supe Culture; Chavín Horizon Sites of the Central Peruvian Coast. *Columbia Studies in Archeology and Ethnology*, vol. III. New York.

The Development of the Formative Culture in the Ceja de Montaña*: A Viewpoint Based on the Materials from the Kotosh Site*

SEIICHI IZUMI
UNIVERSITY OF TOKYO

I. INTRODUCTION

THE study of the Formative culture in the coastal region of the Central Andes might be said to have attained distinction in the 1950's. Rafael Larco Hoyle tried to establish a chronology for the Pre-Columbian cultures in northern Peru through a typological study of the ceramics from the Chicama Valley on the north coast of the Central Andes (Larco 1941, 1944, 1945a, 1945b, 1946, 1948). Paralleling and succeeding this study, a general investigation of the Virú Valley was planned and conducted by the Andean Institute of the United States. The group of archaeologists who were engaged in this excavation included Wendell Bennett (1950),* Junius Bird (1948), Donald Collier (1955), James Ford and Gordon Willey (1949), and William Strong and Clifford Evans (1952). This group achieved success in the investigations at Ancón and Supe on the central coast (Willey and Corbett 1954) and in the Casma Valley (Collier 1943), the Chancay Valley (Willey 1943; Collier 1960), and the Ica Valley (Strong 1957). Other work was done by the Peruvian archaeologist Julio C. Tello, who conducted excavations in the Nepeña Valley (1942, 1943), the Casma Valley (1956), and in the Paracas Peninsula (1959). Frédéric Engel also had an interesting excavation at Curayacu (1956).

Through the above-mentioned series of excavations in the coastal region, the chronology of the coastal Formative culture has been clarified, with each of its phases being represented by abundant cultural contents. The chronology discloses that in the north sedentary agricultural village culture with pottery and maize, i.e., Formative culture, probably began about 1500 B.C., followed around 300 B.C. by the Classic stage or Early Intermediate Period, and that the whole Formative Period was divided into the three phases of early, middle, and late. This chronology was determined mainly by the

* Dates in parenthesis indicate publication, here and throughout.

changes in the types of pottery. The Middle Formative is represented by the Chavín Horizon. The Late Formative is distinguished from this by the appearance of White-on-Red and Negative painted pottery, as well as by the sudden decrease of incised pottery. The division between the middle and early phases, however, seems to be full of ambiguities. The points of reference are so-called Chavín style decoration and polished pottery, and in not a few cases the division between the two phases tends to be chronologically unclear.

As to the Formative culture both on the eastern slope of the Andes, which is geographically called the Ceja de Montaña, and in the Montaña, the following excavations provided materials: in the north at Kuntur Wasi by Rebeca Carrión Cachot (1948); in the central highlands at Chavín de Huántar as well as in the Callejón de Huaylas by Bennett (1944) and Tello (1960); in the central highlands by Augusto Cardich (1964); in Ayacucho by José Casafranca (1960); and down in the south at Chiripa by Bennett (1936); in the Titicaca basin by Alfred Kidder II (1943); in the Cuzco region by John

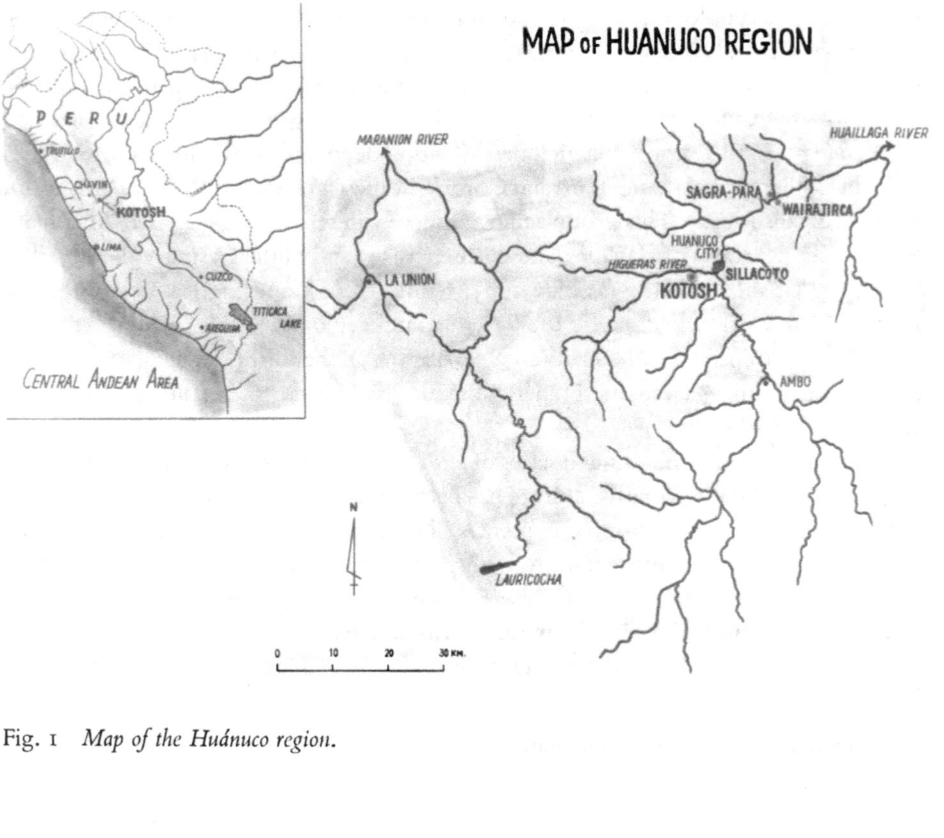

Fig. 1 *Map of the Huánuco region.*

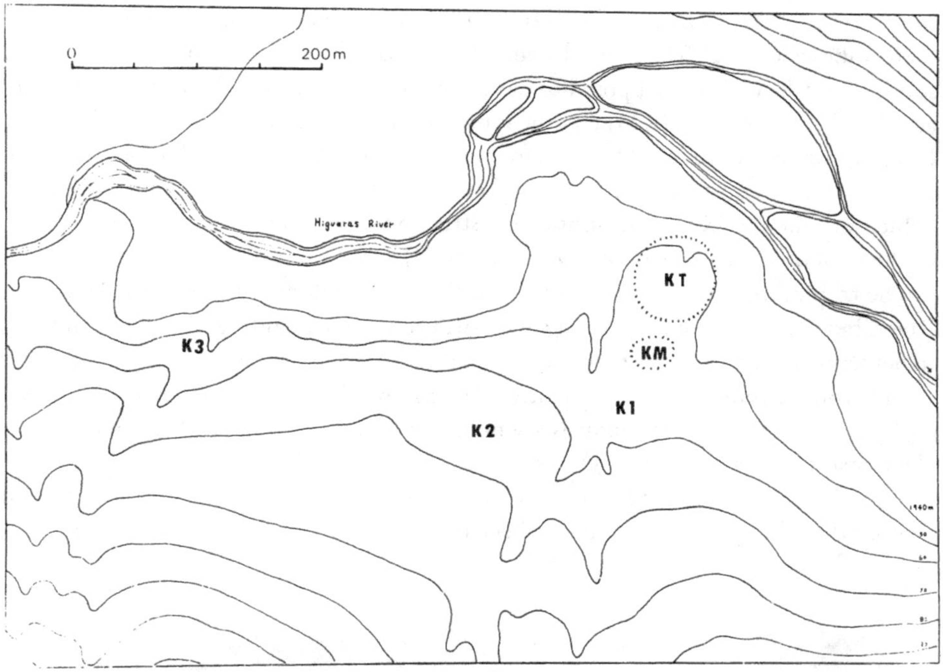

Fig. 2 *The Kotosh site.*

Rowe (1944); and most recently at the Tiahuanaco site by the Bolivian government. In addition, investigations of the Montaña areas have been widely carried out by Donald Lathrap (1958; Lathrap and Roys 1963). However, many of these sites in the Montaña and Ceja de Montaña areas were single occupation sites and therefore it was difficult to do a stratigraphic study in spite of the great number of investigations and excavations. Consequently, the chronology of the Formative cultures in these areas proposed in the 1950's was by no means complete.

I have been interested in the origin and development of the Chavín civilization as the most integrated civilization in the Middle Formative Period in the Central Andes, and I was especially interested in stratified sites in the Montaña or Ceja de Montaña region (Fig. 1), rather than in the coastal region where a sharp contrast cannot be found between the early and middle periods. One such site I had in mind was Kotosh, situated five kilometers west of the modern city of Huánuco in the central part of the Ceja de Montaña region. The site is composed of two artificial mounds and three stone constructions on a lower terrace along the right bank of the Higueras River, a tributary of the Huallaga River. The height of the bigger mound (called KT), from the bottom of the *quebrada* floor which lies to the west, measures 13.7 meters, its summit being 1,961.4 meters above sea level. The mound is cut into two parts by a big trench (KTH) running south to north, which is supposed to have been made by treasure hunters a long time ago. The smaller mound (KM) is to the south of KT, and measures 9.7 meters in height. It was apparently untouched by treasure hunters. South of KM extend stone constructions (K1) of unknown use, and on a higher terrace to the west of the mounds stands a habitation-like site (K2), with another construction group suggesting a cemetery (K3) to the west of it across a narrow *quebrada* (Fig. 2).

The tropical forest begins only thirty to thirty-five kilometers down the Huallaga River, but the area around the site is a semi-arid zone almost without rainfall from May to September. As to the vegetation, here and there in the lower basin along the river are found tropical thorn forests and cultivable land, but the zone from there up to the highlands of 3,800 meters height is a semi-desert area with thorny plants like cactus, algarroba, and huarango (Fig. 3).

The scholar who first paid special attention to the importance of the Kotosh site was Tello, who visited it in 1935 and collected sherds from the surface. He wrote that

Fig. 3 *Ecological view of the Kotosh site (crossing point of the two arrows is KTMound of the site).*

at Kotosh "a ceramic type which imitates wooden vessels in form and ornamented with incised decorations is found in layers lower than those which contain Chavín and Marañon-type sherds" (Tello 1942: 710). Two years after Tello's visit, Collier came to the site and his observations were communicated to Willey, who writes as follows: "[Collier] collected a sample of fifty sherds from the mound surface and from old excavations. These correspond closely to the types which Tello has illustrated plus smooth plain and polished monochrome types. Although Collier describes rim and shape forms as 'suggesting the Chavinoid range,' he found no Classic Chavín designs nor any painted ware" (Willey 1951: 128).

I visited the site in 1958 and, realizing its importance, organized the University of Tokyo Scientific Expedition to the Andes. We carried out large-scale excavations three times, in 1960 (Izumi and Sono 1963), 1963, and 1966. We laid stress on the excavations of the western half of Mound KT, and further excavated part of the KM, K2, and K3 sites. Along with this, several other sites on the upper Huallaga River were excavated. They include Sillacoto, Paucarbamba, Waira-jirca, Sajara-patac (sometimes called Sagra-para), and Piquimina. A series of these excavations made clear that the stratigraphy at Mound KT represents the possible chronology of the Formative cultures in the upper Huallaga basin. Therefore, in the following pages I would like to explain the general features of the co-relations and cultural contents of each of the periods at the Kotosh site.

II. THE CHRONOLOGY AND CULTURAL CONTENTS AT THE KOTOSH SITE

1. *The Kotosh Higueras Period and its Culture* (Fig. 4)

This is a phase widely distributed on the surface of the mounds at Kotosh with ruined constructions and artifacts which are different from those in the foregoing periods. Stone walls and floors of the constructions are plastered with clay. In the interior of the rooms stand monoliths of sericite schist. Burials are usually found under the walls and floors of the constructions, and bodies are flexed on the side. The pottery type representing the period is named Higueras Red. The surface is not well polished and is of red or red-brown color. Most specimens are undecorated; however, some have appliqué designs. Higueras Red shows a variety of shapes: short-necked jars, bowls, and, infrequently, effigy pots. A few specimens of Higueras Red are decorated with negative painting and white-on-red techniques (Kotosh White-on-Red). The copper objects are delicately made, and along with these are found numerous needles, pins with special decorations, bells, and *tupos* (pins with disk-shaped heads or their variations). Other artifacts discovered are T-shaped stone axes, polished stone points, bone artifacts, and

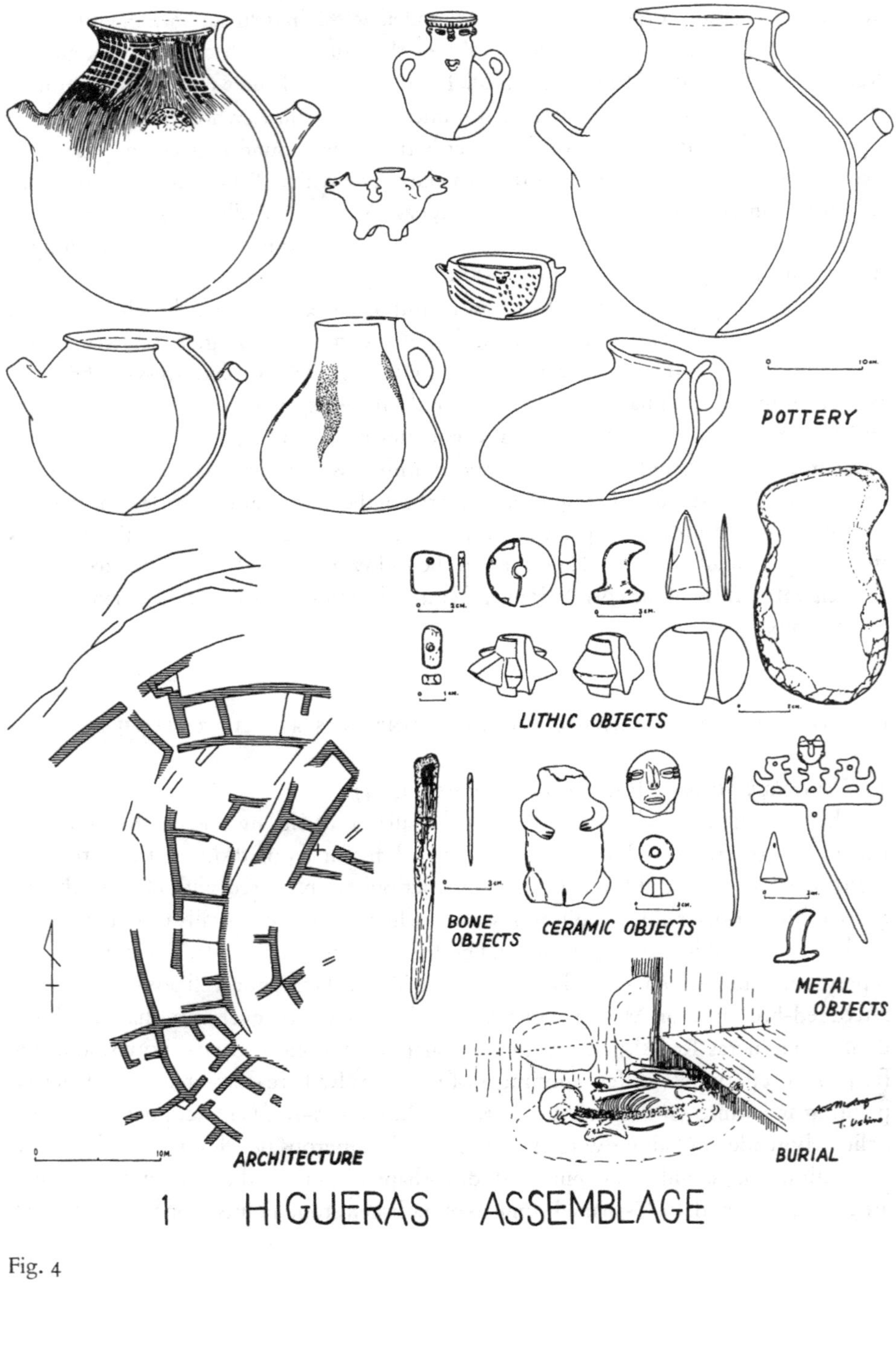
POTTERY
LITHIC OBJECTS
BONE OBJECTS
CERAMIC OBJECTS
METAL OBJECTS
ARCHITECTURE
BURIAL
1 HIGUERAS ASSEMBLAGE

Fig. 4

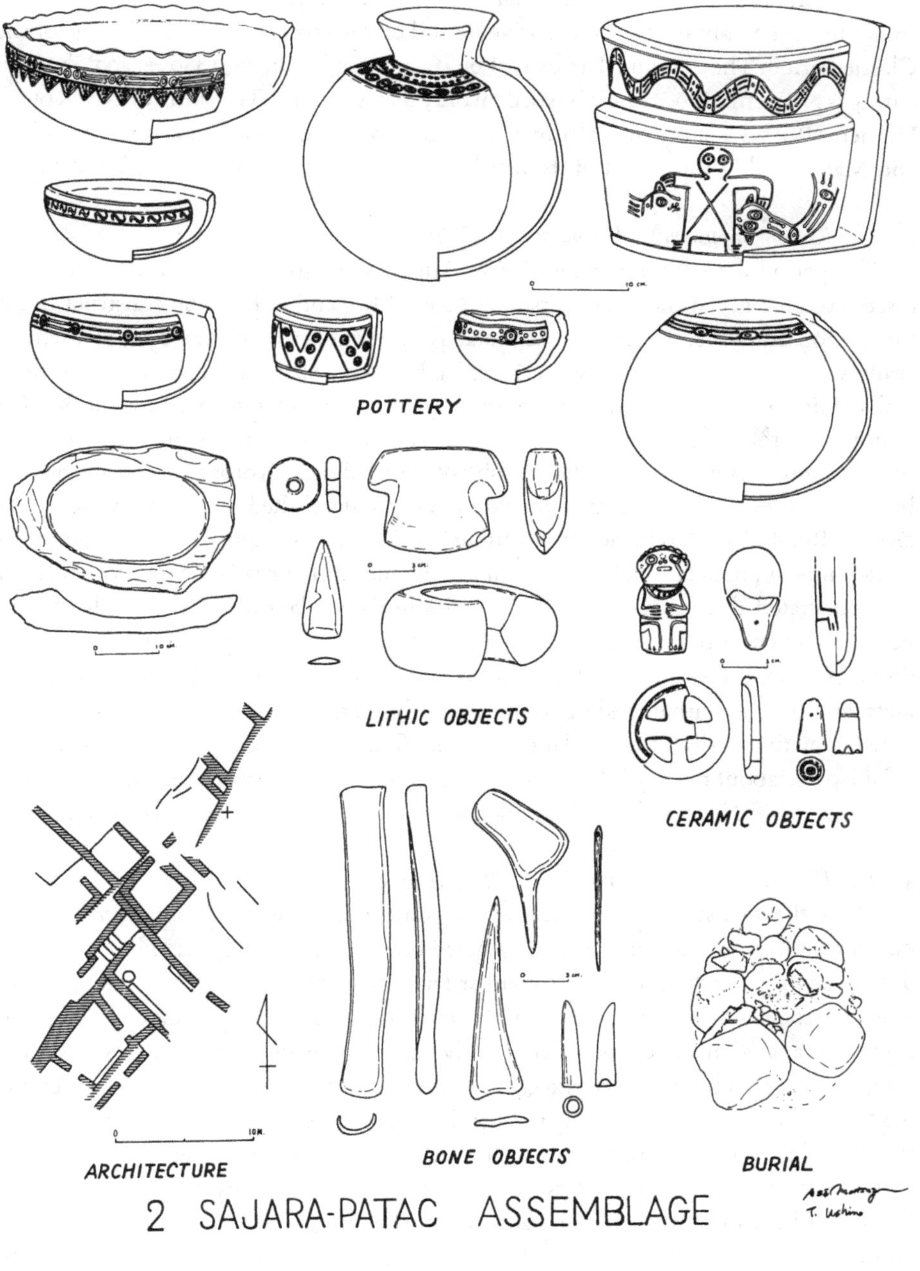
POTTERY
LITHIC OBJECTS
CERAMIC OBJECTS
ARCHITECTURE
BONE OBJECTS
BURIAL
2 SAJARA-PATAC ASSEMBLAGE
T. Ushino

Fig. 5

personal ornaments of various materials. The Kotosh Higueras Period seems to correspond to the late phase of the Formative Period on the coast or to the early stage of the Classic Period. The absolute date by carbon-14 analysis is A.D. 70 (1880 ± 200), but this dating is problematic because it is based on only one specimen. The culture of the Kotosh Higueras Period seems to have formed a horizon over wide areas in the upper Huallaga and Marañón, but the extent of its distribution remains to be investigated in detail.

2. *The Kotosh Sajara-patac Period and its Culture* (Fig. 5)

This period is found under the Kotosh Higueras Period and the constructions are discovered mainly at the western part of Mound KT and at K2. The constructions in this period are a succession of rectangular rooms, and in many cases supplementary walls, which are surmised to have been used as built-in benches, are attached to the main walls. The entrance is located on the short side of the rectangular construction. The majority of the ceramics excavated are bowls and jars with swollen rims, chocolate brown in color and with a polished finish. We labeled them Kotosh Chocolate Brown. In the upper level are found ceramics with red slip and polished surface; they are named Kotosh Red Polished. The design motifs are mainly the combinations or repetition of circle-and-dot, punctation, broad-line incision, and short broad-line incision between two punctated dots; a few cases of incised animal or plant designs were also found. Feline motifs and other Chavín-style decorations are never found. Other specimens discovered are a few copper objects, gold objects, bone artifacts, polished stone artifacts, and personal ornaments. The culture of this period evidently corresponds to the Late Formative Period, and similar cultures are found from Paucarbamba, Waira-jirca, Sajara-patac about twenty kilometers east of Kotosh, and also from San Blas near Junín (Kroeber 1944; Nomland 1939). No definite data for absolute dating was obtained.

3. *The Kotosh Chavín Period and its Culture* (Fig. 6)

This is the only stratum at Kotosh whose content had already been well known, and our chronology at Kotosh is primarily based on it. People in this period seem to have destroyed the preceding constructions in order to build new and bigger buildings. Walls made of stones and clay are covered with a coating to which red paint is applied. Other things excavated are a section of one of the large stairways and what was possibly a temple with two bodies of sacrificed babies beneath its floor. Unfortunately, Trench KTH, which was probably dug by treasure hunters at a later time, completely destroyed the central part of the construction of this period. Some of the ceramic specimens have feline motifs or other typical Classic Chavín decorations; they are classified as Kotosh-Well-Polished. Bone and gold artifacts are also found. Most of the stone artifacts are polished. The artifacts excavated indicate that the Kotosh Chavín culture can be con-

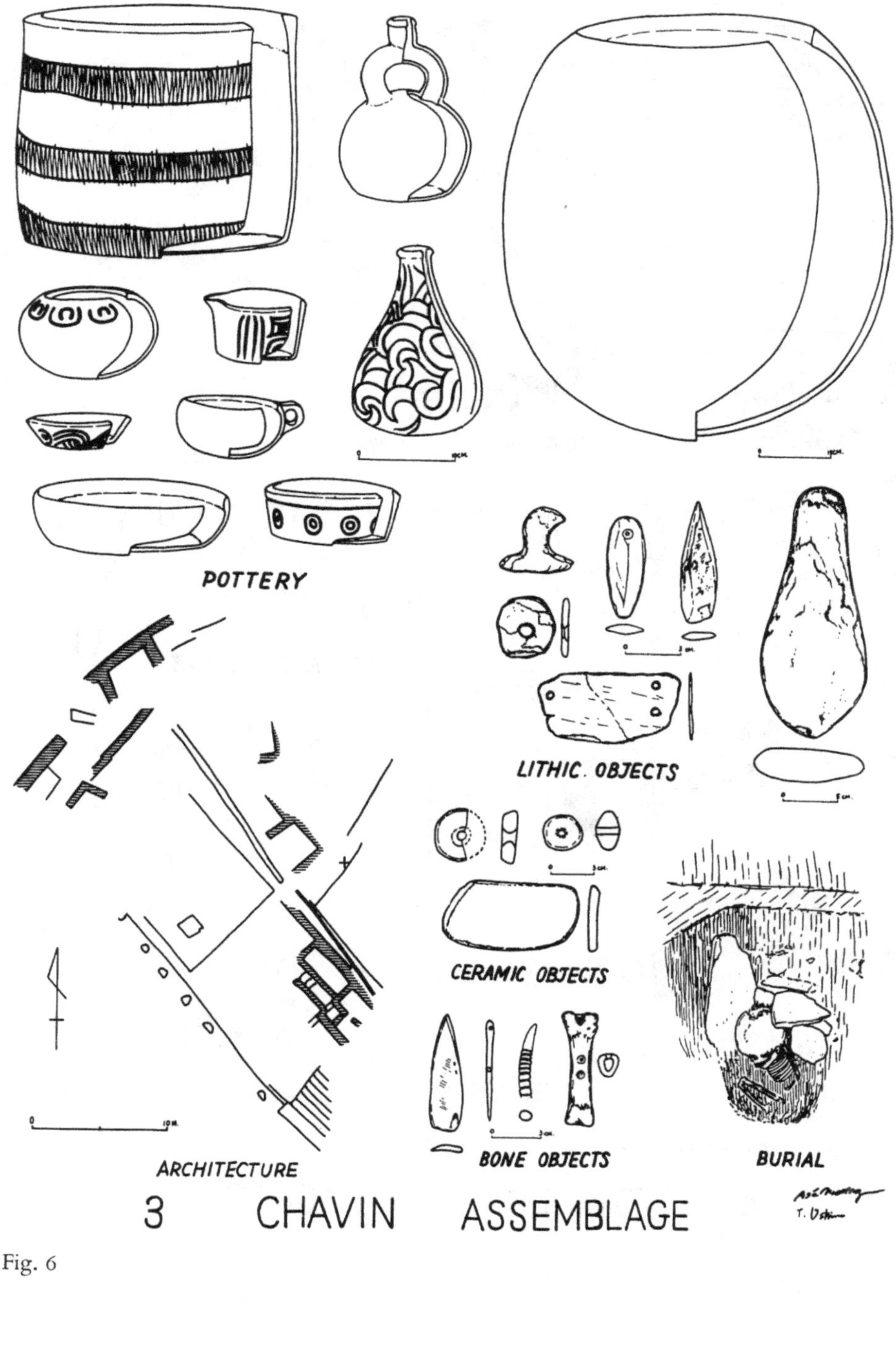
POTTERY
LITHIC. OBJECTS
CERAMIC OBJECTS
ARCHITECTURE
BONE OBJECTS
BURIAL
3 CHAVIN ASSEMBLAGE

Fig. 6

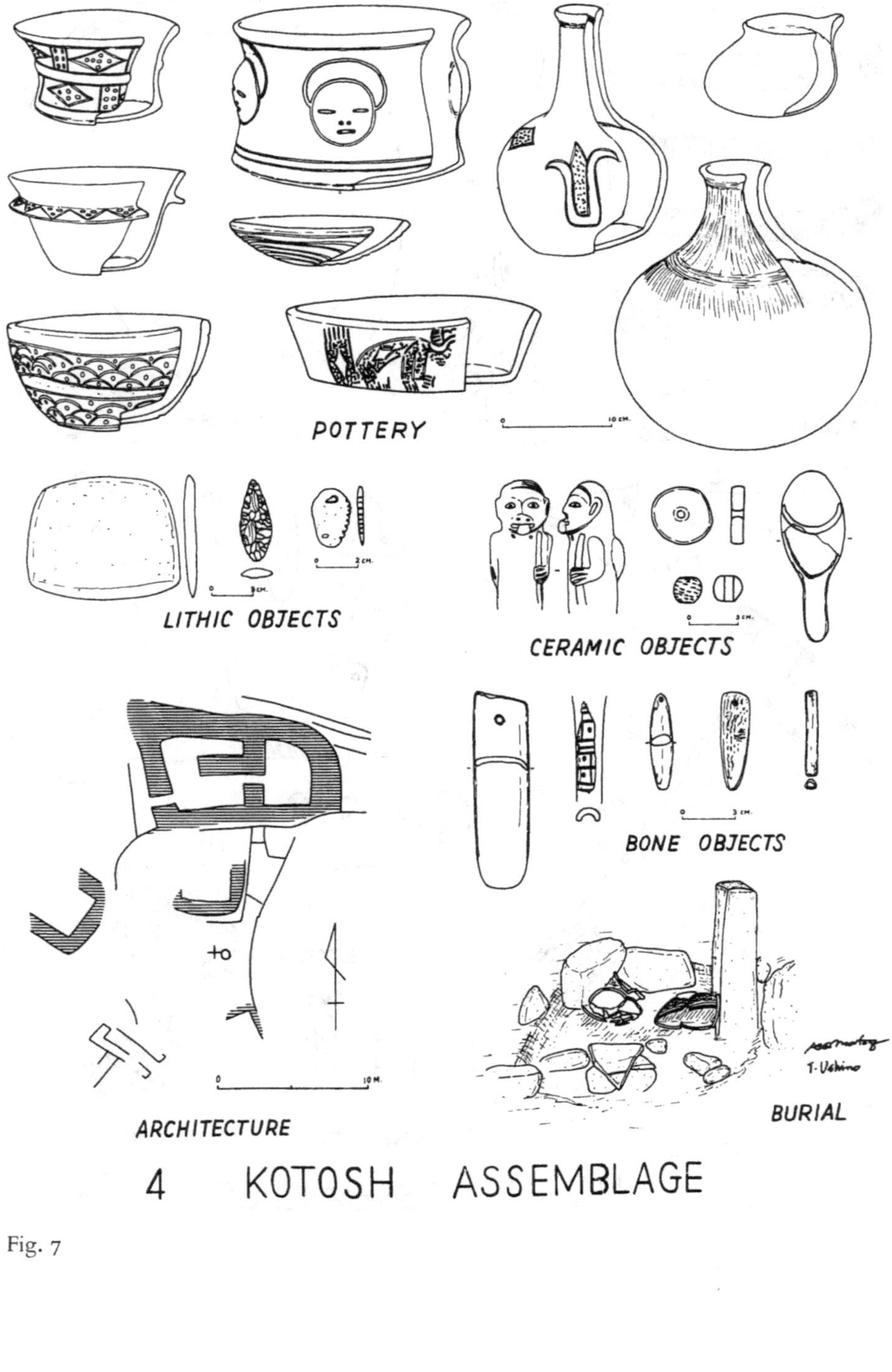
POTTERY
LITHIC OBJECTS
CERAMIC OBJECTS
BONE OBJECTS
ARCHITECTURE
BURIAL
T. Ushino
4 KOTOSH ASSEMBLAGE

Fig. 7

sidered with good reason as the typical Middle Formative culture, that is, the Chavín culture. Among the cultural elements of the Chavín culture lacking at Kotosh are reliefs on the walls of the constructions and stone sculpture. We have two carbon-14 dates for this period, 870 B.C. (2820 ± 120, N–65–2) and 1200 B.C. (3150 ± 150, GAK–263).

4. *The Kotosh Kotosh Period and its Culture* (Fig. 7)

This period appears stratigraphically just under the Kotosh Chavín Period. Carbon-14 datings for this period are 890 B.C (2840 ± 170, N–67–2), 920 B.C. (2870 ± 230, N–66–a), and 1120 B.C. (3070 ± 110, GAK–261) and these show the closeness of this period to the Kotosh Chavín Period. The constructions at Mound KT are too fragmentary to represent the characteristic traits of this period. Secondary burials were evidently executed. At Mound KT three headless bodies were discovered in the floor of the construction surmised to be a temple, and at Sillacoto a human head was discovered in a stone cist. The pottery is distinct from that of Classic Chavín in shape, color, decoration technique, and design motif. The pottery of this period, called Kotosh Grooved, is characterized by carinated bowls with convex sides and bowls with lateral flanges, well-polished red-brown color, plain rocker-stamping, filling of ground with red, yellow, and white colors after firing, and painting with some fugitive black material, possibly graphite. Not many feline motifs appear on the pottery and bone objects. The absence of metal objects and the existence of chipped stone points are the characteristics of this period. The introduction of maize as a staple crop seems to have occurred in this period at Kotosh. As far as we know now, the distribution of Kotosh Kotosh traits is restricted to various sites along the upper Huallaga basin; indications of the same culture are faintly detectable on the pottery fragments obtained by surface collection in the city of Huaraz in the Callejón de Huaylas, in Chavín de Huántar, and in Cajamarca. I am of the opinion that the Kotosh Kotosh Period roughly corresponds to the Early Formative Period in the coastal region; it could also be taken as a transitional stage from the Early to the Middle Formative.

5. *The Kotosh Waira-jirca Period and its Culture* (Fig. 8)

This is the phase beneath the stratum of the Kotosh Kotosh Period. It is the oldest ceramic period at Kotosh. The characteristics of construction remain ambiguous. Placed in the center of a room was a structure composed of three or four stones, possibly used as a fireplace, usually accompanied by floors covered with a quantity of ash. The pottery is represented by the Kotosh Incised type and although a number of ceramics have much in common with those from the Kotosh Kotosh Period, the ones of this period are generally dark brown in color and unpolished. The shapes of the pottery include boat-shaped and triangular bowls, sometimes with protuberances (frequently

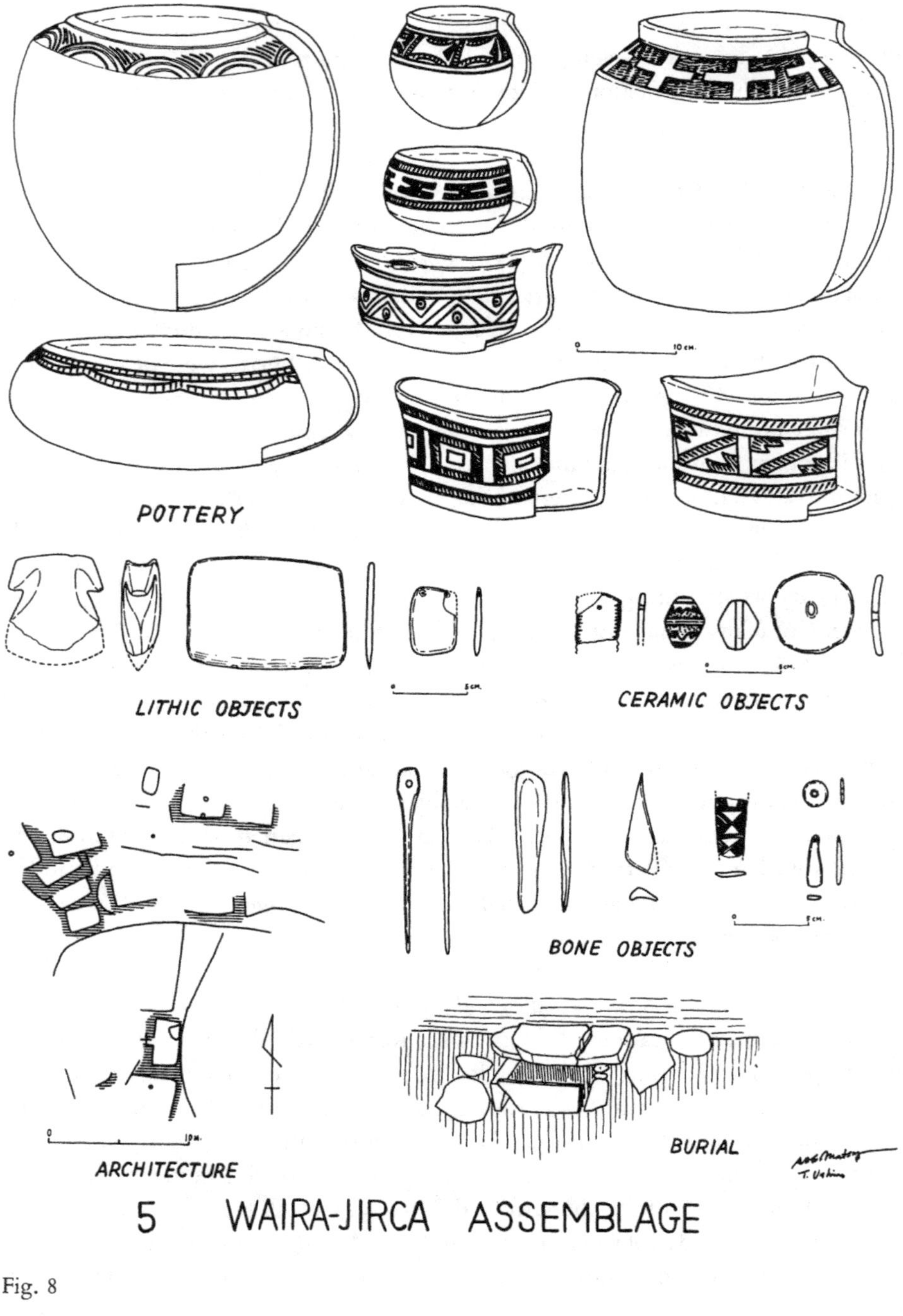
POTTERY
LITHIC OBJECTS
CERAMIC OBJECTS
BONE OBJECTS
ARCHITECTURE
BURIAL
5 WAIRA-JIRCA ASSEMBLAGE

Fig. 8

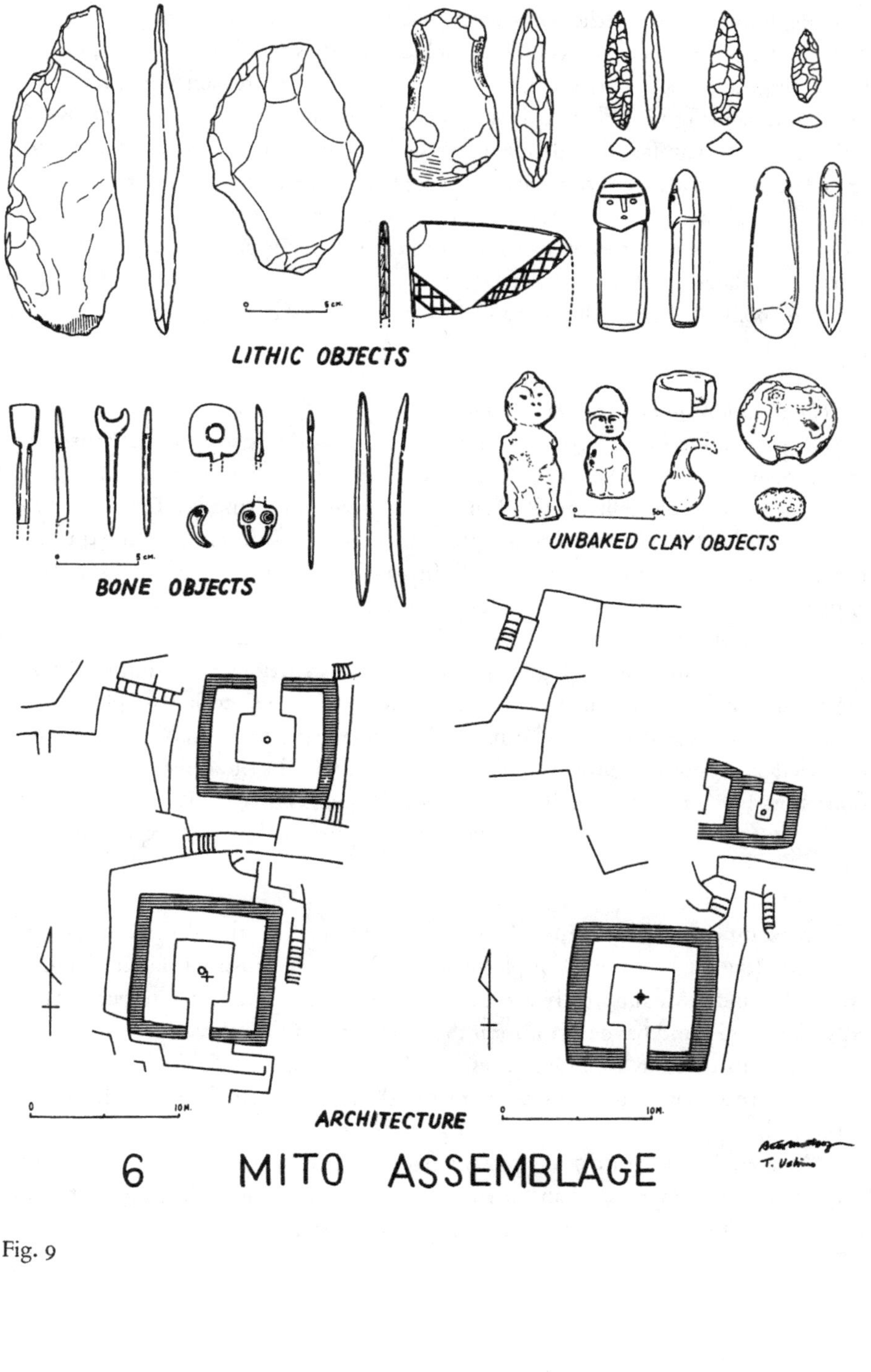

LITHIC OBJECTS
BONE OBJECTS
UNBAKED CLAY OBJECTS
ARCHITECTURE
6 MITO ASSEMBLAGE
T. Uchino

Fig. 9

showing human faces) on the walls, characteristics which are never found in the Kotosh Kotosh Period. Decoration technique includes various types of incision, punctation, burnishing, and in some cases plain rocker-stamping. Graphite painting never exists but post-fired painting with three colors of red, yellow, and white was in wide use. Bone artifacts were manufactured deliberately, but, needless to say, metal artifacts do not exist. As to lithic artifacts, there are more chipped stone points than in Kotosh Kotosh and fewer polished axes. In contrast to the Kotosh Chavín phase, the distribution of the Kotosh Waira-jirca cultural traits is restricted to the upper part of the Huallaga River. Carbon-14 dates for this period are 1850 B.C. (3800 ± 110, GAK–262) and 1830 B.C. (3780 ± 90, GAK–765); this allows us to locate the Waira-jirca culture in the Early Formative.

6. *The Kotosh Mito Period and its Culture* (Fig. 9)

The excavation in 1960 confirmed that a construction existed under the stratum of the Kotosh Waira-jirca Period. The construction had a relief of crossed hands on the wall (Fig. 10), so we called it the Templo de las Manos Cruzadas. From the stratum containing the Templo, not a single piece of ceramic was found, and the quantity of remains that was found was quite small. In 1963 the Expedition group excavated the entire Temple (Fig. 11), and also discovered the Templo de los Nichitos. In 1966, when we dug the northern part of the Templo de las Manos Cruzadas and Mound KM to the south, the Templo Blanco (Fig. 12) and seven constructions and additional artifacts were found in the strata which we called Kotosh Mito. The Kotosh Mito phase does not seem to have extended over the upper Huallaga region, according to our present knowledge. There are, however, pre-ceramic temples in the coastal region, such as those now being investigated by Engel (1966). It may clarify the relationship between these two areas to illustrate in detail the materials obtained by our Expedition.

a. Constructions

The examples are the Templo Blanco (Figs. 11 and 12), the Templo de las Manos Cruzadas (Figs. 10–12), the Templo de los Nichitos, six constructions at Mound KT, two at Mound KM, and finally two at the Waira-jirca site. These constructions of the Kotosh Mito Period have in common the following characteristic traits.

i. The constructions are more or less quadrangular, and inside the walls of the four sides there are large niches extending from the floor and small ones in the middle of the walls.

ii. As is shown in Figure 9, the passage from the entrance and the central part of the floor are one step lower than the surrounding floor. Small niches are built into the low walls supporting the upper floor, except in the Templo Blanco.

iii. In the center of the lower floor there is a fireplace dug on the same level as the surface of this floor, and from the bottom of the fireplace runs a ventilation canal or chimney under the floor.

iv. Final coating is applied to the whole surface of walls and floors.

b. Clay artifacts

Among pieces of baked clay in the refuse heaps of the Templo de las Manos Cruzadas, two baked figurines were found. Both figurines are of a simple type with a body consisting of a flattened lump of clay in the shape of a stick, a face with eyes represented by punctation, and an appliqué nose. In addition to these figurines an unidentifiable object with punctation was found.

Fig. 10 *Relief of crossed hands.*

Fig. 11 *The Templo de las Manos Cruzadas (upper) and the Templo Blanco (lower).*

In the Templo Blanco we discovered unbaked clay objects: a clay disk on the floor, and, in the niches located at the north wall of the Templo, various artifacts including two specimens of figurines, one small vessel, and one imitation of a plant. Neither figurine has hands or feet. Eyes and noses are represented by punctation and some part

Fig. 12 *The Templo de las Manos Cruzadas and a type specimen of the Templo Blanco.*

of the face is painted red. In the pieces of clay found near the figurines can be detected representations of hands and feet, which apparently formed portions of the abovementioned figurines. A design is incised on the surface of the disk, but what it might represent is difficult to tell.

c. Stone artifacts

Most are chipped points, including some leaf-shaped ones, of silicic and hard sandstone. In addition to the points are found a great number of lumps of stone taken to be flakes and cores of various sizes. There are some artifacts of uncertain shape made of big flakes with worked edges.

Stone axes, partially or entirely polished, and chisel-like stone axes are also found. The latter have heads, both sides of which are notched.

Besides the above-mentioned stone tools, stone figurines and decorated stone disks were unearthed. The stone figurines are from Mound KT; they were made with simple incision on sericite schist. Two disks with design motifs were also found, one on the floor of the Templo de las Manos Cruzadas and another from Mound KM. Both of them are polished stone slates with incised geometric motifs.

d. Bone and shell artifacts

Bone and shell artifacts excavated are abundant, as the following specimens show: bone beads, a pipe-like bone with holes, needles with decorated heads, small bone buttons, button-like shell objects, bone disks with holes (which might have been used as parts of spindle whorls), and finally personal ornaments made of polished spiral shell which came from the construction in the north part of Mound KT.

e. Organic remains

Various carbonated seeds are being subjected to an expert analysis by the staff of the New York Botanical Gardens. A great many animal bones are now under examination at the Natural History Museum of the University of Florida. With the exception of animal bones, remains from this period are not very abundant. However, together with the constructions they are important materials for the understanding of the culture. Carbon-14 dating from the Kotosh Mito Period is varied from one material to another, but as far as our present knowledge is concerned, 1950 B.C. can be considered an acceptable date since two laboratories have reported the same results (3900 ± 100, GAK–766B; 3900 ± 900, TK–44).

7. *The Chronology at Mound KT and its Relations with the Surrounding Sites*

The chronology thus established at Mound KT has been validated by the new data from the excavations at Mound KM, at K2 and K3, and also at Sillacoto, Paucarbamba, Waira-jirca, Sajara-patac, and Piquimina. The stratigraphical sequence of the six phases at Mound KT is not always present at all the other sites. The following is a diagram showing the arrangements of the phases at the other sites in comparison with the stratigraphy at Mound KT.

TABLE I Stratigraphies of the Sites in Upper Huallaga Valley

	Kotosh			Other Sites				
Phases at KT	KM	K 2	K 3	Silla-coto	Paucar-bamba	Waira-jirca	Sajara-patac	Piqui-mina
Higueras	O	Δ	O	O	X	X	X	X
Sajara-patac	Δ	O	O	X	Δ	O	O	Δ
Chavín	Δ	X	X	X	O	X	O	Δ
Kotosh	O	X	X	O	X	O	X	X
Waira-jirca	O	X	X	O	X	O	X	X
Mito	O	X	X	O	X	O	X	X

O shows the existence of constructions and other remains
Δ shows the existence of remains unaccompanied by constructions
X absent

The first fact to be noted from the diagram is that the order of the stratigraphical sequence established at Mound KT is basically applicable at the other sites, and the second fact is that the sequence of phases at each site shows certain characteristic patterns.

The Higueras phase does not seem to be closely related to the preceding phase. The culture of this phase does not seem to have spread to the lower part of the Huallaga River beyond the city of Huánuco. The Sajara-patac and Chavín phases show three cases of association. The dating for Mound KT confirms that the Kotosh Chavín period is close to the Kotosh Kotosh period, although in the stratigraphy the latter phase is older than the former. The same cannot be observed at the other sites, which, however, show cases where the Kotosh phase is overlying the Waira-jirca phase in a stratigraphical sequence. Finally, the most interesting fact is that the Mito phase never exists alone without being followed by the Waira-jirca phase. No cases have been reported in which the Mito phase is found on the surface of the site. Some sites of the Mito phase are found from a few meters to some tens of meters under the surface of the earth; therefore, even if there are single Mito phase sites, surface observation would not reveal their existence. To sum up, the Mito phase has some stratigraphical relationship with the Waira-jirca phase, and yet they are interpreted to be chronologically and culturally differentiated from each other. We have found at Kotosh that cultural contents and stratigraphic relations of phases are invaluable in the study of the process of culture.

III. ON THE CHAVÍN CIVILIZATION IN THE CEJA DE MONTAÑA AREA

One phase at Kotosh and other sites along the upper Huallaga basin can be called

Chavín according to Willey's definition of the Chavín style as being characterized by artifacts of stone, pottery, bone, and metal in the style resembling the designs of the stone sculpture at Chavín de Huántar (Willey 1951: 138).

The details of the construction of the Chavín phase at Mound KT are not obtainable because treasure hunters have destroyed an important part of it, but it is clear that the construction is larger in size and better planned than any of those of the other phases. There might have been big steps at the front of the construction leading to the top of the temple, as at the Castillo at Chavín de Huántar. That there are no stone sculptures accompanying the construction is a remarkable point of departure from Chavín de Huántar. The pottery is of the type called Classic Chavín, and some is rendered with feline, bird, or geometric motifs. A feline motif might be attributable to Phase C of the Chavín style, that is, the Ocucaje Phase 3 classified by Rowe and others (Rowe 1962; Menzel, Rowe, and Dawson 1964). For the metal artifacts, dating is impossible, because those from Kotosh have no decorations of any phase of the Chavín style.

As has been pointed out, three phases older than the Chavín phase have been found along the upper part of the Huallaga River, and following is the comparison between each of them and the culture of the Chavín phase.

The double floor of the Mito phase seems to have had some relationship to the floor of the Chavín phase, and the chimney under the floor is somewhat related to the ventilation canal of the Chavín period. But the tradition of the Mito phase construction does not seem to have been handed down to the Waira-jirca and Kotosh phases. Among the stone artifacts, chipped stone points continue to exist from the Mito phase to the Chavín phase although with some variations in their form. Polished stone axes with notched heads appear in both the Mito and Kotosh phases. In the Chavín phase they appear in the form of T-shaped stone axes, which continue to the Higueras phase. In the Mito phase the reliefs of the crossed hands of men and women are found under the niches, forming an important element in the construction. A human figurine of unbaked clay was deposited in a niche. These anthropomorphisms appear to have been a central motif of the Mito phase culture.

As far as we know from our excavations, the Waira-jirca phase has no distinctive structures which serve the comparative study of construction. In regard to stone artifacts, no new type worthy of mention has emerged. The pottery of the Waira-jirca phase is too delicately manufactured to be classified as the oldest type in the Andes. Many of the forms and techniques of this phase are handed down to the Kotosh and then to the Chavín phase; for example, broad-line incision, punctation, plain rocker-stamping, and post-fired painting continue to exist from the Waira-jirca to the Chavín phase. Unlike the Mito phase, no decorations in the construction are reported from the Waira-jirca phase. Clay female figurines, however, were manufactured, indicating that the anthropomorphic objects which were the central motif of the Mito phase were gradually replaced by a "feminine" or "maternal" motif.

As far as the dating is concerned, the Kotosh phase is close to or parallel with the Chavín phase. Some of the decorative motifs on pottery or bone artifacts resemble those of the Chavín style. The central motif for pottery or human figurines is a goddess, and a few cases of feline, bird, and cloud-shape motifs are reported. In this phase, an epoch-making change in production method, that is, the introduction of maize agriculture, took place and, with it, an agricultural cult of human sacrifice was initiated. In some parts of the coastal region, only in the Chavín phase did maize begin to be cultivated, but in the upper Huallaga area the same phenomenon occurred in the Kotosh phase.

TABLE 2 Some Cultural Elements in Formative Periods of Upper Huallaga

	Periods					
Elements	Higueras	Sajara-patac	Chavín	Kotosh	Waira-jirca	Mito
Chipped stone points			O	O	O*	O*
Polished stone axes with notch on the head	O	O	O	O	O	O
Stone metates	O	O	O	O	O	O
Polished stone knives				O	O	O
Polished stone points	O	O	O*	?		
Broad-line incision		O*	O	O*	O	
Punctation	O	O*	O	O*	O	
Plain rocker-stamping			O*	O	O	
Dentate rocker-stamping			O*			
Post-fired painting			O	O*	O*	
Graphite-like painting			O	O*		
Crossed hands motif						O
Anthropomorphic motif	O	O		O	O	O
Maternal motif				O*	O	
Birds motif	O	O	O*	O		
Feline motif			O	O		
Cloud shape motif			O	O		
Step design		O		O	O	
Metal works	(C) (G)	(C) (G)	(G)			

O Shows existence
O* shows remarkable existence
(C) shows the existence of copper tools
(G) shows the existence of gold artifacts

I am not of the opinion, however, that the Kotosh culture is a full-fledged precursor of the Chavín civilization. At various sites along the upper Huallaga, as soon as the Chavín period begins, new cultural elements suddenly emerge: metal artifacts, polished stone points, and various decorations on pottery, all of which are never found in the preceding periods. There are also large-scale constructions built after the destruction of those of the preceding periods. It is not conceivable that so many new cultural elements emerged spontaneously in the upper Huallaga area. We must also hypothesize the existence of other cultures which might have integrated to form the Chavín civilization. The Kotosh phase is one of the many elements that prepared the way.

Finally, I would like to mention the later development of Chavín civilization in the Ceja de Montaña area. At the Kotosh site the Chavín phase is followed by the Sajara-patac phase. The shapes of pottery and the cultural elements in the Sajara-patac phase definitely show its affinity with the Chavín civilization. However, the Chavín-style decorations disappear in this period and geometric motifs come to be dominant. There is only one figurative motif, a hero conquering a monster. He might be viewed as a culture hero with a possible relationship to the stone figures of the periods from the later Formative to the Classic in the Huaylas region, the Casma Valley, and Pucará in the south. It should not be forgotten that copper artifacts appear first at this phase.

The Higueras cultural traits are related to the Sajara-patac ones, but many cultural elements of the Higueras period come from the other regions. For instance, negative painting on pottery and the white-on-red technique do not have their origin in the upper Huallaga. Also as to copper artifacts, influences from some other areas must be taken into account, at least in regard to shapes. The people of the Higueras period might very well have formed numerous big villages but they could not develop to the level of the superb Classic cultures like the Mochica, Nazca, and Classic Tiahuanaco. Only with the Inca invasion did the cultural stagnation of the Higueras period end. I would like to find another opportunity to think about reasons why the superior Formative culture in the upper Huallaga area could not develop to the level of the Classic cultures.

BIBLIOGRAPHY

Bennett, Wendell C.

1936 Excavations in Bolivia. *Anthropological Papers of the American Museum of Natural History*, vol. xxxv, part iv. New York.

1944 The North Highlands of Peru; Excavations in the Callejón de Huaylas and at Chavín de Huántar. *Anthropological Papers of the American Museum of Natural History*, vol. 39, part 1. New York.

1950 The Gallinazo Group, Virú Valley, Peru. *Yale University Publications in Anthropology, no. 43.* New Haven.

Bird, Junius B.
1948 Preceramic Cultures in Chicama and Virú. *In* A Reappraisal of Peruvian Archaeology. *Memoirs of the Society for American Archaeology*, no. 4, pp. 21–28. Menasha.

Cardich, Augusto
1964 Lauricocha, Fundamentos para una Prehistoria de los Andes Centrales. *Studia Praehistórica*, vol. iii. Centro Argentino de Estudios Prehistóricos, Buenos Aires.

Carrión Cachot, Rebeca
1948 La cultura Chavín: dos nuevas colonias, Kuntur Wasi y Ancón. *Revista del Museo Nacional de Antropología y Arqueología*, vol. 2, no. 1, pp. 99–172. Lima.

Casafranca, José
1960 Los nuevos sitios arqueológicos chavinoides en el Departamento de Ayacucho. *Antiguo Perú, espacio y tiempo*, pp. 325–333. Lima.

Collier, Donald
1955 Cultural Chronology and Change as Reflected in the Ceramics of the Virú Valley, Peru. *Fieldiana: Anthropology*, vol. 43. Chicago.
1962 Archaeological Investigations in the Casma Valley, Peru. Akten des 34. Internationalen Amerikanistenkongresses, pp. 411–417. Horn-Vienna.

Engel, Frédéric
1956 Curayacu—a Chavinoid Site. *Archaeology*, vol. 9, no. 2, pp. 98–105. Brattleboro.
1966 Le complexe précéramique d'El Paraiso (Pérou). *Journal de la Société des Américanistes de Paris*, vol. lv, no. 1, pp. 43–96. Paris.

Ford, James A. and Gordon R. Willey
1949 Surface Survey of the Virú Valley, Peru. *Anthropological Papers of the American Museum of Natural History*, vol. 43, part 1. New York.

Izumi, Seiichi and Toshihiko Sono
1963 Andes 2. Excavations at Kotosh, Peru, 1960. Tokyo.

Kidder, ii, Alfred
1943 Some Early Sites in the Northern Lake Titicaca Basin. *Papers of the Peabody Museum of American Archaeology and Ethnology, Harvard University*, vol. xxvii, no. 1. Cambridge.

Kroeber, Alfred L.
1944 Peruvian Archaeology in 1942. *Viking Fund Publications in Anthropology*, no. 4. New York.

Larco Hoyle, Rafael
1941 Los Cupisniques. Lima.
1944 Cultura Salinar. Buenos Aires.
1945a La cultura Virú. Buenos Aires.
1945b Los Cupisniques. Buenos Aires.
1946 A Culture Sequence for the North Coast of Peru. *In* Handbook of South American Indians. *Bureau of American Ethnology, Bulletin 143*, vol. 2, pp. 149–175. Washington.
1948 Cronología arqueológica del norte del Perú. Buenos Aires.

Lathrap, Donald W.
1958 The Cultural Sequence at Yarinacocha, Eastern Peru. *American Antiquity*, vol. 23, no. 4, pp. 379–388. Salt Lake City.

LATHRAP, DONALD W. and LAWRENCE ROYS

1963 The Archaeology of the Cave of the Owls in the Upper Montaña of Peru. *American Antiquity*, vol. 29, no. 1, pp. 27–38. Salt Lake City.

MENZEL, DOROTHY, JOHN H. ROWE, and LAWRENCE E. DAWSON

1964 The Paracas Pottery of Ica: A Study in Style and Time. *University of California Publications in American Archaeology and Ethnology*, vol. 50. Berkeley and Los Angeles.

NOMLAND, GLADYS A.

1939 New Archaeological Site at San Blas, Junín, Peru. *Revista del Museo Nacional*, vol. 8, pp. 61–66. Lima.

ROWE, JOHN HOWLAND

1944 An Introduction to the Archaeology of Cuzco. *Papers of the Peabody Museum of American Archaeology and Ethnology, Harvard University*, vol. XXVII, no. 2. Cambridge.

1962 Chavín Art: An Inquiry into its Form and Meaning. The Museum of Primitive Art, New York.

STRONG, WILLIAM D.

1957 Paracas, Nazca and Tiahuanacoid Cultural Relationships in South Coastal Peru. *Memoirs of the Society for American Archaeology*, no. 13. Salt Lake City.

STRONG, WILLIAM D. and CLIFFORD EVANS, JR.

1952 Cultural Stratigraphy in the Virú Valley, Northern Peru. *Columbia Studies in Archeology and Ethnology*, vol. IV. New York.

TELLO, JULIO C.

1942 Origen y desarrollo de las civilizaciones prehistóricas andinas. Reimpreso de las Actas del XXVII Congreso de Americanistas de 1939. Lima.

1943 Discovery of the Chavín Culture in Peru. *American Antiquity*, vol. 9, no. 1, pp. 135–160. Menasha.

1956 Arqueología del Valle de Casma. Culturas: Chavín, Santa o Huaylas Yunga u Sub-Chimú. Publicación Antropológica del Archivo "Julio C. Tello" de la Universidad Nacional Mayor de San Marcos, vol. I. Lima.

1959 Paracas. Primera parte. Publicación del Proyecto 8b del Programa 1941–42 de The Institute of Andean Research de New York. Lima.

1960 Chavín. Cultura matriz de la civilización andina. Primera parte. Publicación Antropológica del Archivo "Julio C. Tello" de la Universidad Nacional Mayor de San Marcos, vol. III. Lima.

WILLEY, GORDON R.

1943 Excavations in the Chancay Valley. *In* Archeological Studies in Perú. 1941–1942. *Columbia Studies in Archeology and Ethnology*, vol. I, pp. 123–196. New York.

1951 The Chavín Problem: A Review and Critique. *Southwestern Journal of Anthropology*, vol. 7, no. 2, pp. 103–144. Albuquerque.

WILLEY, GORDON R. and JOHN M. CORBETT

1954 Early Ancón and Early Supé Culture: Chavín Horizon Sites on the Central Peruvian Coast. *Columbia Studies in Archeology and Ethnology*, vol. III. New York.

The Tropical Forest and the Cultural Context of Chavín

DONALD W. LATHRAP
UNIVERSITY OF ILLINOIS

At the onset of any discussion of the Chavín Horizon, it is well to acknowledge our debt to Julio C. Tello. Our concept of Chavín as an horizon style or a basic cultural tradition has been pruned and refined by later scholars (Willey 1951; Rowe 1962), but it was Tello who first recognized Chavín as a cultural unit, who first perceived the seminal effects of Chavín on a wide range of later Central Andean styles, and who first placed Chavín in its proper chronological position (Tello 1943; 1960). Later studies, with their more restrictive definitions and more precise methods, have tended to focus our attention on the various flaws in Tello's interpretations. From time to time it is well to view Tello's writing in terms of the breadth and correctness of the general picture he was painting rather than to dwell on the mistaken details, which are understandable considering the limited data which Tello had at his disposal.

In a discussion specifically oriented to the influence of the *selva* on Chavín and the relationship between the Chavín Horizon cultures and Tropical Forest cultures, it is particularly appropriate to do homage to Tello. One could present his views on this question at length, but I will confine my comments to one specific contribution that he made in this area. It was Tello who first discovered the Kotosh site in the Huánuco basin. At Kotosh he isolated as a distinct ceramic style the materials we now call Kotosh Waira-jirca, and suggested the possibility of a Tropical Forest derivation for this style (Tello 1943: 152, Pl. XIX b) (Fig. 2). It is important to emphasize that Tello was the first to isolate a ceramic style which we now know to be of Initial Period date. In a recent book, Edward P. Lanning (1967: 21) erroneously granted this priority to Gordon R. Willey and Marshall T. Newman.

If we wish to ask the question, "To what degree did the tropical forest environment and/or specific Tropical Forest cultures contribute to the pattern we call Chavín?"; we must first answer the question, "Where and when did Chavín first crystalize as a cultural pattern?" Up till now, I have seen nothing approaching a definitive answer to this second question. Lanning (1967: 100, 107) is certainly correct in pointing out that the Chavín style is intrusive into such central highland sites as Kotosh and into such central coast sites as Curayacu and the Tank Site. The north coast valleys such as

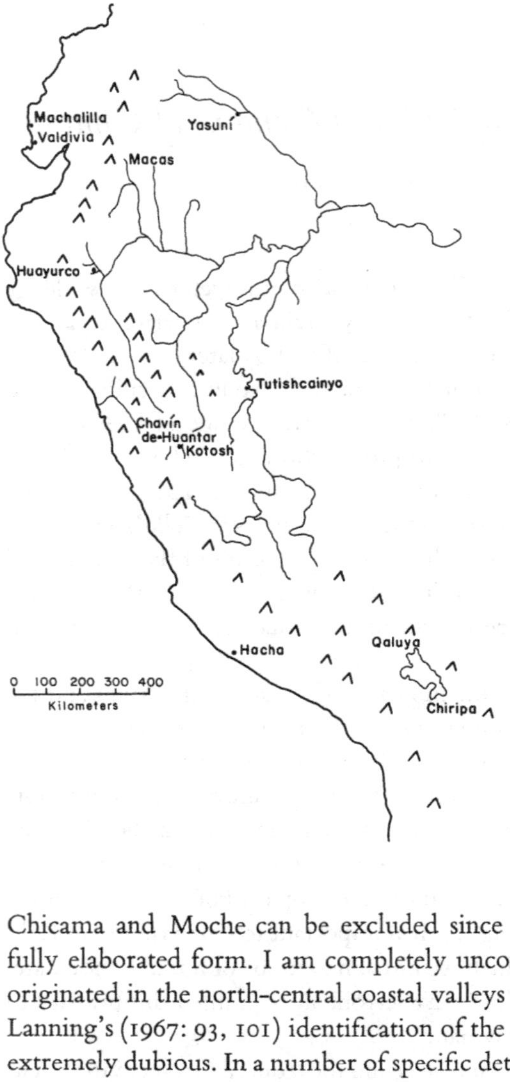

Fig. 1 *Map of west-central South America showing the location of some of the archaeological zones and sites significant to the discussion.*

Chicama and Moche can be excluded since Chavín art never occurred there in a fully elaborated form. I am completely unconvinced by the argument that Chavín originated in the north-central coastal valleys such as Casma or Nepeña. I think that Lanning's (1967: 93, 101) identification of the Cerro Sechín carvings as pre-Chavín is extremely dubious. In a number of specific details the Cerro Sechín carvings suggest a rustic rendering of the EF segment of Rowe's (1962) chronology for Chavín rather than a precursor of Chavín AB.

If we reject the north-central coast as the hearth for the Chavín style we must conclude that Chavín initially developed either in the highlands or on the eastern slopes of the Andes and that the southernmost possible hearth for Chavín art is the site of Chavín de Huantar itself. There is *no* reason to exclude the highlands farther to the north as a possible point of origin; the internal chronologies of the two other major highland sites, Kuntur Wasi and Pacopampa, should be examined carefully before they are rejected. Until the forested, eastern slopes of the Andes have been examined as carefully as have the highland basins and coastal valleys, we had best not dismiss this region *ex cathedra* as Lanning has recently done (1967: 100).

I strongly suspect that the fauna depicted in Chavín art give some kind of clue about the homeland of the people who developed this art. I am convinced that the felines depicted are jaguars and that the snakes are certainly constrictors, most likely anacondas. Anacondas have a far more restricted range than jaguars, occurring only within the flood plains of the major rivers in the tropical lowlands east of the Andes. I am furthermore convinced that Rowe (1962: 18) and Yacovleff (1932) are correct in identifying the birds depicted in Chavín art as eagles. The massive tarsi, the total conformation of the talons, the markedly recurved bill, and the indication of an erect fringe of feathers on the head and neck all argue that it is an eagle which is being depicted in most instances.

Fig. 2 *Sherds of the Kotosh Waira-jirca Period illustrated by Tello* (1943: Pl. XIXb).

We may further ask, "What species of eagle is being depicted?" If one consults the magnificently illustrated *Birds of Prey of the World* (Grossman and Hamlet 1964), direct comparisons can be made between the various bird elements used to build up Chavín designs and each of the species of eagle occurring in South America (Fig. 3). The beak of the harpy eagle, *Harpia harpyja*, shows by far the best correspondence with the beaks depicted (Grossman and Hamlet 1964: 161). It is exceptionally massive; the tip is as fully recurved as in the Chavín convention; there is a very large, tooth-like projection near the base of the upper mandible (a feature typical of Chavín beaks); and there is a sharp demarcation between the upper mandible and the cere, which makes the Chavín convention of treating the cere and nostril as a scroll understandable. The magnificent crest of the harpy eagle is a plausible model for the series of scrolls which

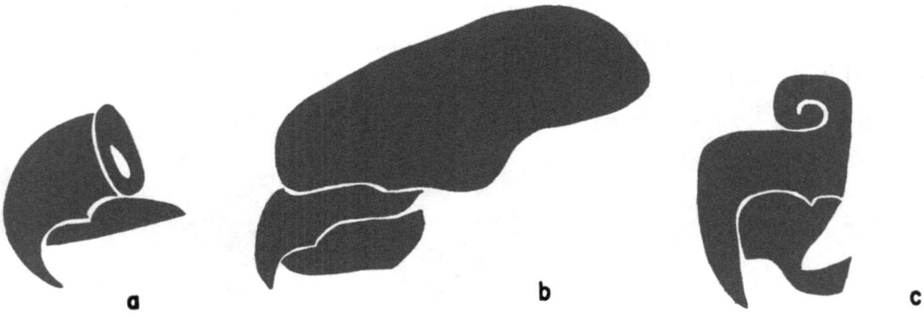

Fig. 3 *Silhouette of the beak and cere of the harpy eagle, a; and silhouette of the beak and carbuncle of the Andean condor, b; compared with a typical Chavín representation of the beak of a raptorial bird, c* (*a* and *b* after Grossman and Hamlet 1964).

crown the head of Chavín eagle depictions, and the massive, partially feathered tarsi of the harpy are only slightly exaggerated in the short, massive tarsi depicted in Chavín eagles.

The black-and-chestnut eagle, *Oroaetus isidori*, is a smaller, less impressive bird, and has a less fully recurved beak and a less marked mandibular tooth, but next to the harpy eagle it is most like the Chavín depictions (Grossman and Hamlet 1964: 299). The solitary eagle *Harpyhaliaetus solitarius*, is the only eagle of the altiplano. Its bill is less massive, less recurved, and lacks the mandibular tooth so clearly depicted in Chavín art (Grossman and Hamlet 1964: 291). The crested eagle, *Morphnus guianensis*, has a far less massive bill than the harpy and its range does not approach the Central Andes (Grossman and Hamlet 1964: 292). Thus, the only likely models for the Chavín eagles are the harpy and the black-and-chestnut. Both are monkey-eating eagles whose habitat is limited by their food preference. The harpy eagle is the typical monkey eater of the Amazon lowlands, while the black-and-chestnut eagle has as its typical habitat the upper *ceja* zone.

The harpy eagle is by far the most impressive and powerful raptorial bird in South America. On a world wide basis its only peer is the monkey-eating eagle of the Philippines. Many of the Tropical Forest tribes held the harpy eagle in great veneration, raising the young for their feathers and for purposes of ceremonial exchange and trade. (The harpy eagle tames well.) It would appear appropriate, considering what we surmise about Chavín ideology, that the attributes of the most powerful known carnivore, the jaguar, were combined with the attributes of the most powerful raptorial bird, the harpy eagle, and the most powerful constrictor, the anaconda.

The natural range of the harpy eagle approaches the eastern slope of the Andes only around the bend of the Marañón. It is completely absent from the Ucayali basin (Grossman and Hamlet 1964: 294). If the harpy eagle is the model for the Chavín eagle, the originators of Chavín art at the very least had trade relations with peoples of the tropical forest, living on the floor of the Amazon basin. The most likely models for the various elements of Chavín iconography are all fauna of the dense tropical forest, and only the jaguar ranges outside that zone. If the originators of Chavín art were not inhabitants of the tropical forest, they were at least remarkably familiar with its fauna, a fact suggesting a greater proximity to that ecological zone than would be afforded by the Casma and Nepeña Valleys.

If we cannot pinpoint exactly where the Chavín culture originated, that is to say, whether in the north-central to northern Andes adjacent to the *selva* or at the eastern foot of the Andes in the *selva* itself, we can at least show that, at the time when Chavín artistic and religious tradition was crystalizing, the *selva* was already occupied by people with an advanced form of Tropical Forest culture.

There is a long cultural sequence now known from the Central Ucayali (Lathrap 1958; 1968; n.d.a; n.d.b), on which I would like to concentrate. This region is within the tropical forest, on the floor of the Amazon basin, less than five hundred feet above sea level, not far east of the highlands. The lower Andean foothills have also been densely occupied by ceramic-using societies for at least the last four thousand years, as indicated by the continuing work of William Allen in the nearby lower *ceja* zone of the Alto Pachitea (Allen n.d.).

The radiocarbon dates relating to the Central Ucayali sequence are presented in Figure 4. They need no special comment, and none of the dates needs to be explained away, as all are in proper stratigraphic order. The shaded bands represent discrete components at various of the sites which have been excavated in the Central Ucayali

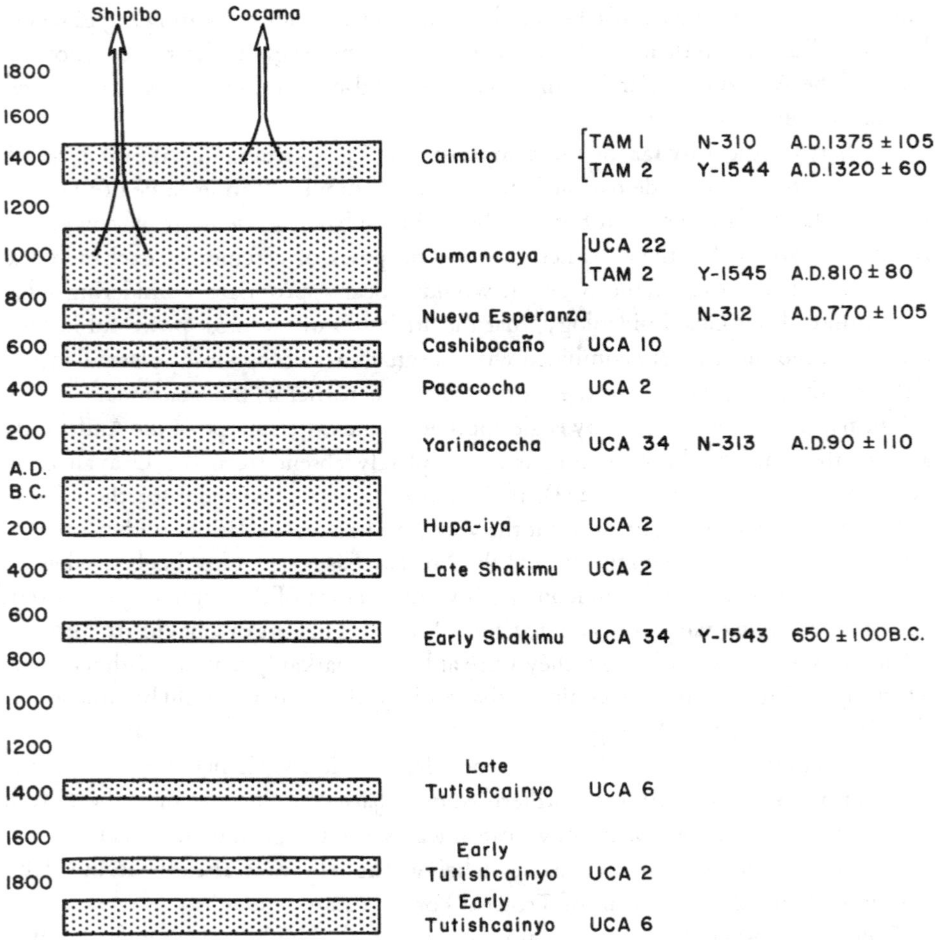

Fig. 4 *The cultural chronology of the Central Ucayali. The shaded bars give estimates of the duration of the various components so far excavated. The names of the cultural complexes are given in the second column, the site designations in the third column, and the available carbon-14 assays in the fourth column.*

basin. The width of the bands indicates an estimate of the duration of each component. Such estimates were arrived at on the basis of a comparison of the thickness of midden for each component with the accumulation rates observable in modern Shipibo villages. Where there are no radiocarbon dates, and in cases where two components are clearly in the same cultural tradition, the duration of the lacuna between the two components is estimated on the basis of the amount of cultural changes occurring between the two components. The basis of these estimates should be discussed in detail.

In those instances where one of the components can be shown to be a direct linear evolution from a previous component in the same cultural tradition, the amount of cultural change separating the two components should have *some* relationship to the amount of time separating them. It can be shown that this condition of relationship holds for the hiatus between Early Tutishcainyo and Late Tutishcainyo, between Late Tutishcainyo and Early Shakimu, and between Early Shakimu and Late Shakimu. There is, on the other hand, a *complete* cultural discontinuity between Late Shakimu and Hupa-iya.

I have followed Evans and Meggers (1960: 241–2), who have suggested that for cultures of roughly similar level it should be possible to establish rates of ceramic change. I have modified their method by concentrating entirely on shape categories, which seem to bear some relationship to the conceptual categories of the people who made the pottery involved, and which permit a greater degree of comparability between the work of various archaeologists.

Between Early Tutishcainyo and Late Tutishcainyo there was a fifty percent replacement of shape categories. If we look at vessel shape categories we find that there are sixteen basic vessel shapes in Early Tutishcainyo (Lathrap n.d.a: Table 142). If we look at Late Tutishcainyo we find that there are again sixteen basic vessel shapes but eight of these vessel shapes are not present in the Early Tutishcainyo sample (Lathrap n.d.a: Table 146). Changing these figures into a statement about popularity of vessels of various shapes, we find that fifty-two percent of the vessels made in Late Tutishcainyo are of forms not present in Early Tutishcainyo. (In achieving these figures there has been some simplification, minor variants in rim profile have been lumped, and there has been no consideration of variation in basal angle for vessels with the same rim profile.)

The Valdivia sequence of the coast of Ecuador offers excellent comparative materials. There are large samples of sherds carefully analyzed as to vessel form and covering a long span of time (Meggers, Evans, and Estrada 1965). The date is presented in a readily usable synoptic form (Fig. 54), which in most respects appears directly comparable to the development from Early Tutishcainyo to Late Tutishcainyo.

Since the sample from the early part of Valdivia Period A is rather small, we will consider the degree of change in shape categories from the latter part of Period A to the end of Period D. Meggers, Evans, and Estrada present twenty-three shape categories for the whole of the Valdivia Phase. Of these twelve, Numbers 1, 2, 3, 4, 5, 6, 7, 11, 13, 14, 17, 18, are demonstrably present in significant numbers toward the end of Period A. Fourteen shape categories are present in significant quantity at the end of Period D, and of these six have survived from the later part of Period A; and eight, Numbers 8, 9, 10, 15, 16, 21, 22, 23, are innovations or major modifications. In contrast to the fifty percent replacement of shape categories between Early and Late Tutishcainyo there is a fifty-seven percent replacement of shape classes from late Period A, Valdivia, to terminal Valdivia D. In terms of the relative frequency of vessels, vessels of the new forms make up about fifty percent of all ceramics present during terminal Valdivia D. The dating of the Valdivia sequence will be discussed below, and it would appear that a conservative estimate of the amount of elapsed time between late A and terminal D would be nine hundred years.

Patterson's study of changes in vessel shape categories for the Miramar-Lima stylistic continuum is more fine grained than either Meggers, Evans, and Estrada or I were able to achieve (Patterson 1966). On the other hand Patterson's samples for the various phases were small, so that quantification of his data is on a less secure basis. Nonetheless, reasonably meaningful comparisons seem possible. In the Base Aérea Phase Patterson recognizes eleven shape categories. In Lima 3, Patterson again recognizes eleven shape categories, fully eight of which represent continuations of shape categories present in Base Aérea with only minor, progressive modification, while three represent innovations, or fissions within previous shape categories. One might argue that Olla 2A in Base Aérea (Patterson 1966: 14, Fig. 2a) is a different shape category than Olla 2B in Lima 3 (Patterson 1966: 52, Fig. 11a), and that there are thus four rather than three replacements. However, the shifts between any two consecutive phases are minute and there is clearly continuity. In terms of the level of discrimination exercised either by Meggers, Evans, and Estrada or by myself, it seems accurate to treat them as a single category. There is thus a twenty-seven percent replacement of shape categories between Base Aérea and Lima 3, and only twenty-two percent of the total vessels represented in the Lima 3 sample are of forms not represented in Base Aérea. Patterson's most conservative estimate of the length of time represented by the Base Aérea-Lima 3 continuum is about 450 years (Patterson 1966: 98–104). Both the Valdivia and Miramar-Lima data suggest a similar rate of change in vessel form, about twenty-five percent for every 450 years expressed either as percent of new shape categories appearing, or percent of total vessels of forms not present at the earlier point in time.

It will be noted that the percentage of change in vessel shape categories between Early Tutishcainyo and Late Tutishcainyo is about equal to that in the nine hundred years of the Valdivia sequence examined, or about twice that of the 450 years of the Early Intermediate sequence on the central coast of Peru. One might argue for a direct application of the rate suggested by the two control cases. I would prefer to be more conservative and halve the rate, suggesting that it would be extremely unlikely if the span of time separating the Early and Late Tutishcainyo components at site UCA-6 were less than 450 years.

I have belabored this point because there seems no other direct way to arrive at an estimate of the age of Early Tutishcainyo and because there has been a tendency in some recent literature (Hilbert 1968: 50–4; Evans and Meggers 1968: 90–2) to minimize the amount of cultural difference between Early and Late Tutishcainyo.

On the basis of the materials excavated in 1956 the stratigraphic relationship between Late Tutishcainyo and Shakimu was clear, but the degree of cultural relationship between the two components was not clear. In an earlier presentation of these materials (Lathrap n.d.a: 212), I was unable to exclude the possibility that Shakimu represented a site unit intrusion from some other area of South America. The excavation of another Shakimu component at site UCA-34, directly across the *caño* from UCA-6 completely clarified the situation. The component from UCA-34, excavated in 1964, will henceforth be designated as Early Shakimu.

Early Shakimu consists of a series of vessel shape categories which have evolved directly from those of late Tutishcainyo (Fig. 5). Typically these vessels are decorated with simple, broadline, incised decoration. The simple design motifs are derived from those of Late Tutishcainyo, but there is absolutely no zoned texturing (Fig. 6). In terms of the amount of modification of vessel shape categories and alterations in rim profiles, the change from Late Tutishcainyo to the Tutishcainyo derived part of Early Shakimu is greater than that between Early Tutishcainyo and Late Tutishcainyo.

Fig. 5 *Typical Early Shakimu form categories, all of which have evolved by gradual modification from form categories present in Late Tutishcainyo. The three forms in the top row average about 20 cm. in diameter.*

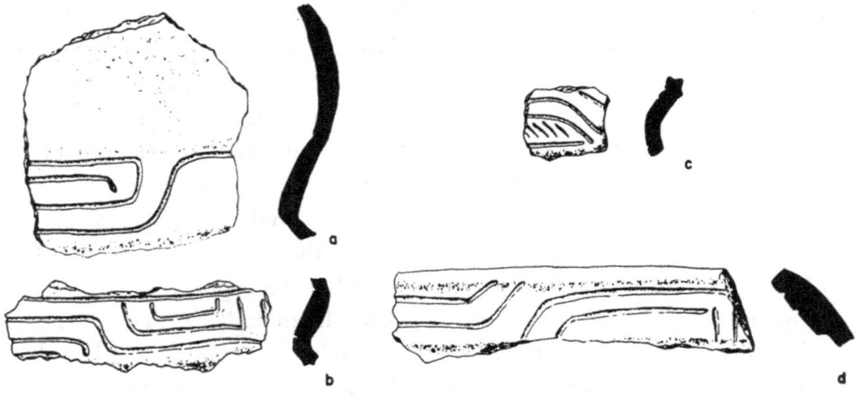

Fig. 6 *Typical Early Shakimu simple incised designs, a,b,d; and Late Tutishcainyo zone-incised sherd, c, showing the motif from which Early Shakimu simple incision evolved.*

To the Tutishcainyo derived part of the ceramic complex have been added four vessel shape categories which are completely alien to the Tutishcainyo tradition. These intrusive shape categories (Fig. 7) are typically decorated with complex designs carefully executed in a combination of incision and excision, and covered by a subsequent application of a thick, highly burnished, dark red slip. In Early Shakimu there is little mixing between these two historically distinct traditions, with simple incision almost never occurring on the exotic vessel forms and excision occurring only rarely on the Tutishcainyo derived forms.

Considering the amount of evolution represented in the Tutishcainyo-derived part of the complex, a span of six hundred years between Late Tutishcainyo and Early Shakimu seems conservative. A radiocarbon assay of 650±100 B.C. (Y-1543) is securely associated with the Early Shakimu component at UCA-34. Between the Early Shakimu component at UCA-34 and the Late Shakimu component at UCA-2 there are major shifts in the popularity of various vessel shape categories, and a complete blending of the two distinct decorative traditions (Lathrap n.d.a: Figs. 56–72). A conservative estimate of the time involved would be two hundred years. The subsequent components in the Central Ucayali sequence have no bearing on the Chavín problem, but their order and the carbon-14 dates associated with them can be read from Figure 4.

In Figure 8 I have aligned the early part of the Central Ucayali sequence with the well described sequence from Kotosh and with the sequence which Meggers, Evans, and Estrada have developed for the early ceramic cultures of the central coast of Ecuador. Brief comments should be made on the dating of each of these sequences and its subdivisions.

Three radiocarbon dates were published in the report on the first season excavations at Kotosh (Izumi and Sono 1963: 154–6). Two of these seem fully acceptable while the third is in poor agreement with the other two and with other published carbon-14 dates for Peru. The earliest dates the Kotosh Waira-jirca Period and suggests it was flourishing by 1850 B.C. A date of about 1050 B.C. for the Kotosh Kotosh Period is fully in accordance with its stratigraphic position. An identical date for the Kotosh Chavín Period seems at least two hundred years too early, in terms of its stratigraphic position at Kotosh, and in terms of the dating of similar manifestations in most other parts of Peru.

The Kotosh Waira-jirca Period at Kotosh encompasses two major construction levels at the site, G and H. The authors of the Kotosh report (Izumi and Sono 1963: 153) claim that there is no difference in the cultural content between the two levels, but this statement appears dubious in terms of the amount of time involved, and in terms of their own published evidence. The most characteristic decorated type in the Waira-jirca phase, Kotosh Incised, shows a considerable range of variation. The zone-incised sherds within this type show two sharply contrasting tendencies. One group, which we will call A, is characterized by evenly executed, closely spaced, diagonal, fineline hatching, executed with some form of stylus (Fig. 2, top row right corner, first three in third row from top, first three in fourth row). The other group, which we shall call B, has more widely spaced incision usually executed with the fingernail (Fig. 2, first three in top row, second and third in second row, fourth in third row). If one plots the distribution of all of the illustrated examples, one notes that Group A is most common in construction level H while Group B is more common in construction level G and later levels (Fig. 9).

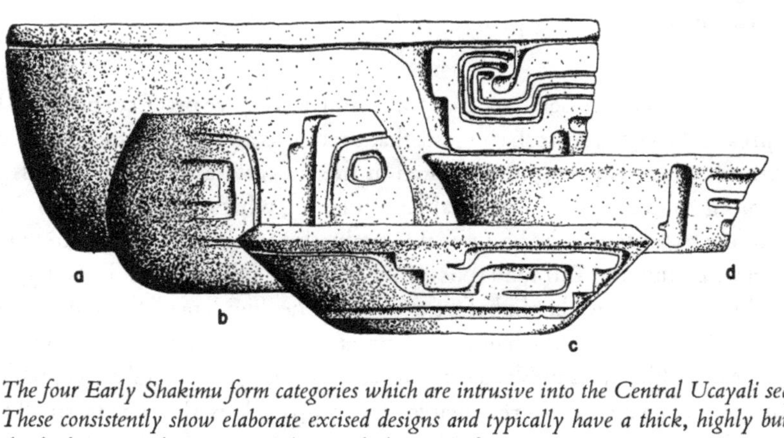

Fig. 7 *The four Early Shakimu form categories which are intrusive into the Central Ucayali sequence. These consistently show elaborate excised designs and typically have a thick, highly burnished slip laid on over the excision. The mouth diameter of c is 20 cm.*

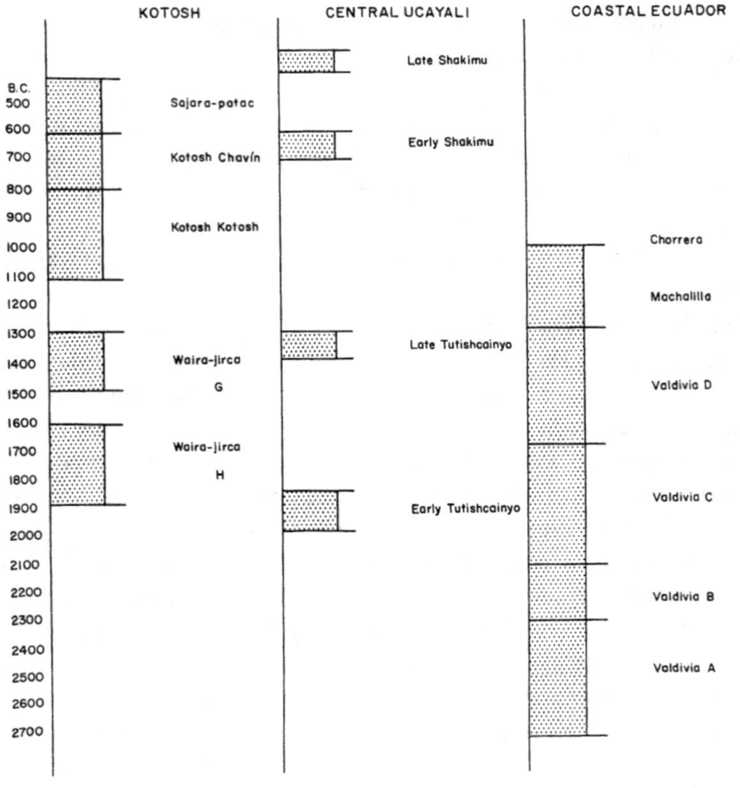

Fig. 8 *Suggested alignment between the Central Ucayali sequence and the sequences of Kotosh and of coastal Ecuador.*

The marked shifts in vessel shape categories and decorative practices between Kotosh Waira-jirca and Kotosh Kotosh suggests that there was an intervening span of cultural development which is poorly represented in the collections so far published.

The dating of the Valdivia-Machalilla sequence, which is presented in Figure 8, appears to me to represent the best possible evaluation of the carbon-14 dates presented by Meggers, Evans, and Estrada (1965: Table G). The full range of dates suggests that Valdivia Period A did not begin before 2700 B.C. The "evidence" for a temporal overlap between Valdivia and Machalilla is completely unconvincing (Lathrap n.d.b: 97). The three Machalilla dates published by the authors seem completely acceptable, and a range of 1300–1000 B.C. seems reasonable and compatible with the very small amount of temporal variation in the phase. The range of data presented by Meggers, Evans, and Estrada seems to me a convincing demonstration that Machalilla is a direct outgrowth of Valdivia D rather than a site unit intrusion. I do not have time to review all of the evidence but will point only to the general continuity of vessel shapes between Valdivia D and Machalilla, and to the close similarity between the Late Valdivia type, Punta Arenas Incised, and the Machalilla type, Machalilla Incised (Meggers, Evans, and Estrada 1965: Cf. Fig. 21.2 with Fig. 80.2).

The dating for Kotosh, Central Ucayali, and coastal Ecuador in each of the three chronological columns has been achieved on internal evidence. It is now time to see if this alignment in Figure 8 makes sense in terms of the evidence for mutual influence.

The relationships between Kotosh Waira-jirca and Early Tutishcainyo are numerous and specific. These mainly relate to Group A of the type, Kotosh Incised, a range of vessels decorated with zone-hatched incision and post-fired crusting. Almost all Kotosh vessels in this category have sharply inflected silhouettes, with a carination dividing the convex hemispherical base from the straight or concave sidewalls (Izumi and Sono 1963: Pls. 136–8). Almost all of these carinated shape categories have precise homologies in the shape vocabulary of Early Tutishcainyo (Lathrap n.d.a: Table 142). The closely spaced, evenly executed, fineline hatching so characteristic of Kotosh Waira-jirca H is identical to the zoned incision of Early Tutishcainyo (Evans and Meggers 1968: Pl. 78). The tradition of post-fired crusting with a hematite paint, probably in a resin base, is shared by Kotosh Waira-jirca H and Early Tutishcainyo. In both instances it is used as an overlay on the areas of fine hatching.

Distribution of Kotosh Zoned Incised Group A

Levels	A	B	C	D	E	F	G	H
	1					9	12	23
							22	23

Distribution of Kotosh Zoned Incised Group B

Levels	A	B	C	D	E	F	G	H
	1	1	1	1	2	9	8	8
							23	8

Fig. 9 *Distribution of the two groups of the type Kotosh Incised, Group A having closely spaced, fine-line hatching, and Group B having widely spaced hatching executed with a fingernail.*

The decorative fields on Kotosh Incised vessels are the same decorative fields habitually used on Early Tutishcainyo vessels. The extreme labial and basal flanges which are so typical of Early Tutishcainyo are absent in Kotosh Waira-jirca H, but there are instances of decoration of the expanded upper surfaces of Kotosh Waira-jirca rims which are a pale reflection of the decorated labial flanges and asymmetrical lip tabs so typical of Early Tutishcainyo (Izumi and Sono 1963: Pls. 137.9, 138.7).

There are some formulae of design layout and some design motifs which are common in Kotosh Waira-jirca H and absent in Early Tutishcainyo, but others are shared in identical form. Of particular interest is the design illustrated by Izumi and Sono (1963: Pl. 138.5). It is of great persistence in the Kotosh sequence lasting through the Kotosh San Blas Period (Izumi and Sono 1963: Pl. 121.9). This motif occurs commonly on the side panels of Early Tutishcainyo vessels (Fig. 10).

Double-spout-and-bridge bottles, in which the high, arched bridge far overtops the short, rather dumpy spouts, are shared by Early Tutishcainyo and Kotosh Waira-jirca (Lathrap n.d.a: Fig. 35h; Izumi and Sono 1963: Pl. 90a.1–5).

The trend from closely spaced, evenly executed fineline incision to more widely spaced and cursorily executed zoned incision, which is evident as one goes from level H to level G at Kotosh, parallels the trend in the development from Early Tutishcainyo to Late Tutishcainyo (Lathrap n.d.a: Fig. 44). Furthermore, Late Tutishcainyo zoned incision and the zoned incision of Kotosh Waira-jirca G tend to occur as narrow, parallel-sided bands extending horizontally around the full circumference of the vessel (Lathrap n.d.a: Fig. 46).

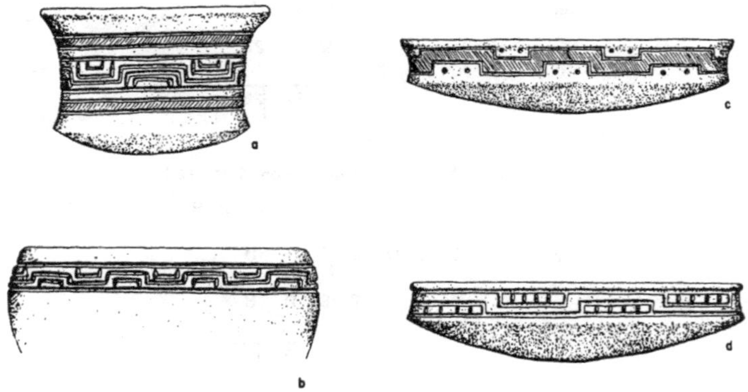

Fig. 10 *Design layout shared by the Kotosh and Tutishcainyo traditions: a Kotosh Waira-jirca; b Kotosh Sajara-patac; c–d Early Tutishcainyo* (a and b after Izumi and Sono 1963: Pls. 138.5; 121.11). *The diameter of c is 20 cm.*

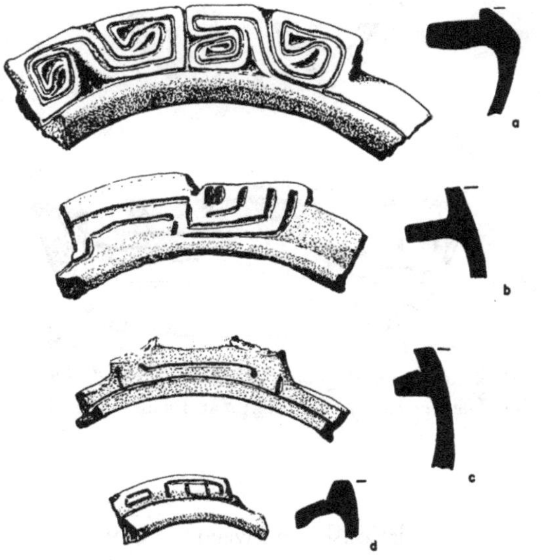

Fig. 11 *Typical sub-labial flanges of the Early Shakimu Complex.*

The Kotosh Kotosh phase appears to have been the cultural climax at that site. There are still a number of cultural traits shared between the Huánuco Basin and the sequence on the Central Ucayali flood plain. The broad, highly decorated, sub-labial flanges which are so conspicuous in Kotosh ceramics, have no parallels in Early Tutishcainyo, but similar decorated flanges occur on about three percent of Late Tutishcainyo vessels (Lathrap n.d.a: Fig. 46e, f, l–p). Such sub-labial flanges continue to be a significant part of the decorative repertory in the Early Shakimu component at UCA-34 (Fig. 11). The extreme carination characteristic of some Kotosh Grooved vessels of Kotosh Kotosh (Izumi and Sono 1963: Pl. 131.1, 2) finds its closest parallel in the profiles of the most common form of Late Tutishcainyo vessel (Lathrap n.d.a: Fig. 40).

Even more striking parallels can be noted between Kotosh Kotosh and the tradition of excised vessels which is intrusive into the Early Shakimu complex. The two most common of these intrusive vessel shape categories are identical in shape, rim profile, and modal size to two common Kotosh Kotosh vessel forms (Izumi and Sono 1963: Pls. 132.11, 14; 135.1; 132.9, 10). Furthermore, in both Kotosh Kotosh and Early Shakimu these forms are typically finished with a heavy, highly burnished red slip, which is laid on over the incised and/or excised decoration. Finally the excised designs which in Kotosh Kotosh only appear on such vessels, are sometimes similar in motif and organization to the excised designs on such vessels in Shakimu (Fig. 12). There can

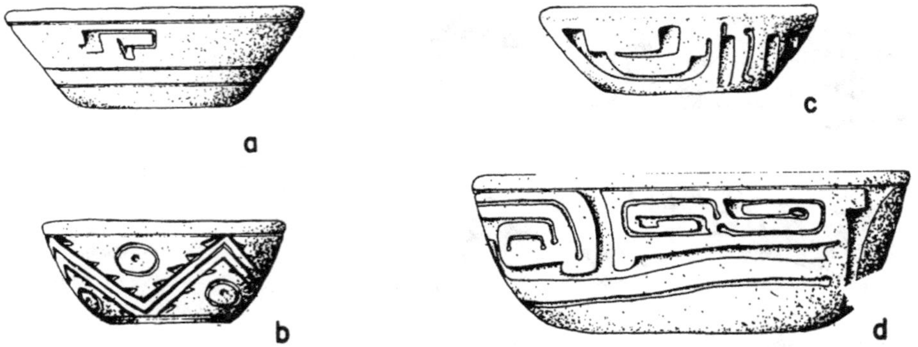

Fig. 12 *Red slipped, excised bowls from Kotosh Kotosh, a–b; and from Early Shakimu, c–d. There is zoned graphite painting on a and b also. The diameter of c is 20 cm.*(*a* and *b* after Izumi and Sono 1963: Pl. 132.14, 9.)

be no doubt about the existence of an historical relationship between these two groups of vessels. The alignment which I have presented would necessitate a spread from the highlands to the Montaña for this last particular set of traits, a matter to which I will return later.

There are convincing parallels in rim profile and vessel form between the Late Shakimu component at UCA-2 and Kotosh Sajara-patac, but subsequently, from the Hupa-iya component up to the end of the sequence, the materials of the Central Ucayali flood plain show no noteworthy similarities to materials in or to the west of the Peruvian and Ecuadorian Andes.

A comparison of the Valdivia-Machalilla sequence with that on the Central Ucayali presents several points of interest. Considering the temporal alignment suggested here, it would be surprising if strong similarities appeared between Valdivia A or B and any part of the Central Ucayali sequence. The zoned crosshatching of Valdivia Fine-line Incised is not similar in style to the zoned hatching of Early Tutishcainyo. On the other hand, vessel shape 11 of the Valdivia sequence (Meggers, Evans, and Estrada 1965: Fig. 54), which appears throughout the seriated Valdivia and Machalilla sequence (form 14 of Machalilla), is probably homologous with the Early Tutishcainyo cup form suggesting that further back in their history Valdivia A and Early Tutishcainyo share a common cultural heritage (Lathrap n.d.a: Table 142.3–4).

The most obvious trend in the development of Valdivia B into Valdivia C and D is the progressive increase in the importance of strongly carinated vessels. By the mid-point of Valdivia C the trend is marked, and there are an ever-increasing number of carinated forms from that point on through Machalilla. Valdivia vessel shapes 8 and 9

(Meggers, Evans, and Estrada 1965: Fig. 54) are the earliest of these strongly carinated forms, and seem to have their closest parallels in Kotosh Waira-jirca form 64 (Izumi and Sono 1963: Fig. 44). Valdivia shape 10, which becomes important in Period D and continues on into Machalilla as an important type, has absolutely no parallels in the Kotosh sequence, but is identical in both profile and size to a common form in Early and Late Tutishcainyo (Lathrap n.d.a: Figs. 31, 45).

The similarities between Machalilla and Late Tutishcainyo are both precise and numerous. Machalilla vessel shapes 4, 6, and 9 (Meggers, Evans, and Estrada 1965: Fig. 90) are identical to common Late Tutishcainyo vessel shapes (Lathrap n.d.a: Figs. 42a, 45a, b) while shapes 1, 2, and 3 differ from Late Tutishcainyo forms only in a slight modification of the rim. A striking feature in both complexes is the insistence on modifying all available carinations and other salient angles of the vessel with nicks or gashes. Meggers, Evans, and Estrada have designated this tendency as Machalilla Embellished Shoulder (1965: Pls. 140, 141) when it occurs alone, but it is typically combined with other decorative techniques on Machalilla vessels. In Late Tutishcainyo this procedure is ubiquitous and occurs in combination with all other techniques (Lathrap n.d.a: Figs. 40a–d; 41d, j; 42c, g, h, etc.). Machalilla Incised open bowls are very similar to the most common style of Late Tutishcainyo open carinated bowl both in vessel profile and in the execution of the design (Cf. Lathrap n.d.a: Fig. 45a, b, with Meggers, Evans, and Estrada 1965: Pl. 144h, Fig. 80.2). The most singular feature shared by Machalilla and Late Tutishcainyo is the purely decorative extra ridge or carination occuring on restricted forms such as bottles and ollas (Meggers, Evans, and Estrada 1965: Figs. 78.8, 85.12). In Late Tutishcainyo this feature occurs on double-spout-and-bridge bottles and other forms (Lathrap n.d.a: Figs. 47g, 49a, 50e).

The stirrup-spout bottles of Machalilla are the earliest so far known, and a good case can be made that this widespread and distinctive ceramic form was "invented" by potters of the Machalilla culture. The peculiar form which the Machalilla stirrup

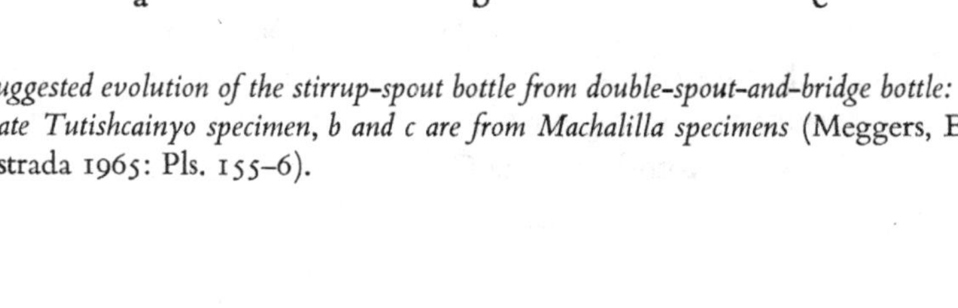

Fig. 13 *Suggested evolution of the stirrup-spout bottle from double-spout-and-bridge bottle: a is after a Late Tutishcainyo specimen, b and c are from Machalilla specimens* (Meggers, Evans, and Estrada 1965: Pls. 155–6).

a b c

Fig. 14 *Zoned reed punctation from Late Tutishcainyo, a–b; and from Machalilla, c* (after Meggers, Evans, and Estrada 1965: Pl. 157°).

spouts assume suggests that the form evolved as a reinterpretation or misunderstanding of the double-spout-and-bridge bottle, a form which has clear priority over the Machalilla stirrup-spout bottles in Hacha, in Kotosh Waira-jirca, and in Early Tutishcainyo. Certain Late Tutishcainyo double-spout-and-bridge bottles, in which the two spouts have moved so close together along the bridge that they have almost merged, offer excellent prototypes for this suggested evolution (Fig. 13).

Zoned reed punctation in sharply angular fields (Fig. 14) is rare in both Machalilla and Late Tutishcainyo, but the few examples in the two complexes look strikingly alike (Lathrap n.d.a: Figs. 49c, 52s; Meggers, Evans, and Estrada 1965: Pl. 157°).

Ayangue Incised, which is characterized by fineline incision in a very dry paste, is the most spectacular decorated type in Machalilla. It has no close parallels in the pottery actually manufactured by the people of Late Tutishcainyo. There are, however, striking parallels in execution, motif, and design layout between Ayangue Incised and Sanidine Tempered Ware, traded in large quantities (fully five percent of all pottery used) to the Late Tutishcainyo peoples (Cf. Lathrap n.d.a: Figs. 54, 55, with Meggers, Evans, and Estrada 1965: Pls. 131–4). Compare especially the use of a small diamond motif with central punctation, stacked rectangles with central punctations, and a jagged step motif (Fig. 15). Sanidine Tempered Ware shows zoned red slip painting, a feature previously absent in the Central Ucayali sequence but important in Machalilla.

Detailed comparisons between the early part of the Central Ucayali sequence and the other two very long and very early sequences available reinforce the dating estimates of the Central Ucayali sequence based on internal evidence. The most striking and convincing comparisons are between Early Tutishcainyo and the H construction level of Kotosh Waira-jirca, between Late Tutishcainyo and Machalilla, and between Early Shakimu and Kotosh Kotosh. These are in proper order and all are compatible with the general arrangement of Figure 8.

The cross-ties between Kotosh and the Central Ucayali sequence are of particular importance since they permit us to include the Central Ucayali materials within the Central Andean cultural chronology, which has been given its most detailed and useful expression by Rowe (1960). It is clear that Early Tutishcainyo is early within the Initial Period, that Late Tutishcainyo is fairly late within the Initial Period, while Early Shakimu and Late Shakimu are within the Early Horizon.

It has long been argued that the Early (Chavín) Horizon was a time of considerable cultural uniformity throughout much of the Central Andes and it is now clear that these uniformities are more numerous and more widespread than the iconography of the Chavín art style as defined in a strict sense (Willey 1951; Rowe 1962). Within the Early Horizon, detailed and highly specific comparisons can be made between Early and Late Shakimu and complexes over much of Peru.

The most typical feature of Shakimu ceramics—a surface slipped with fine-grained materials and then brought to a high, even gloss through intensive burnishing—is also typical of much Early Horizon pottery in the Central Andes, particularly that bearing Chavín iconography. This is true of Kotosh Well Polished (Izumi and Sono 1963); the materials from Chavín de Huantar itself (Tello 1960); the Chavín materials from the

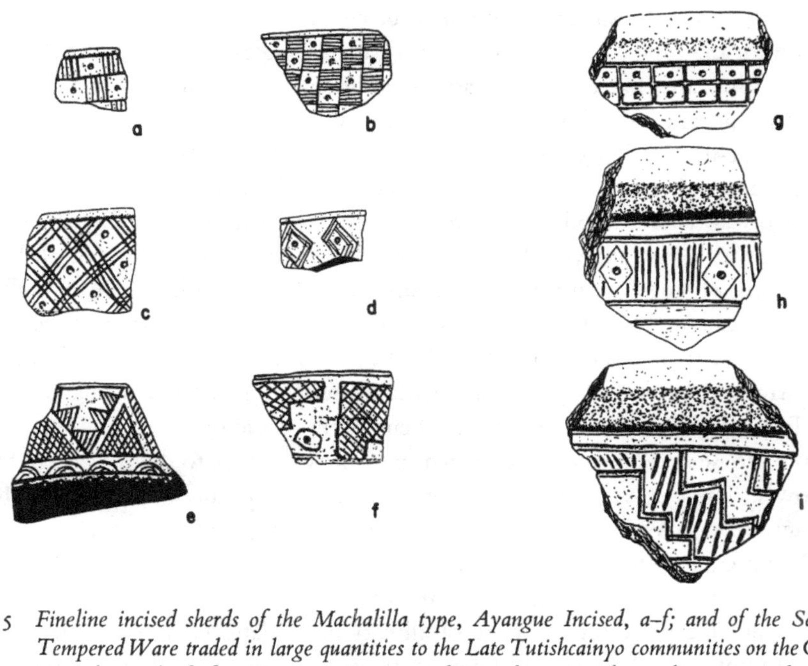

Fig. 15 *Fineline incised sherds of the Machalilla type, Ayangue Incised, a–f; and of the Sanidine Tempered Ware traded in large quantities to the Late Tutishcainyo communities on the Central Ucayali, g–i* (a–f after Meggers, Evans, and Estrada 1965: Pls. 134b, c; 133a, d; 131m; 133r).

Callejón de Huaylas (Vescelius, personal communication 1964); Cupisnique; the Chavín materials at the the Tank Site and Curayacu (Willey and Corbett 1954; Engel 1956; Lanning n.d.); and the South Coast manifestations showing Chavín influence (Menzel, Rowe, and Dawson 1964). It is also true of south highland ceramics of Early Horizon date, such as Qaluyu, which are innocent of any specific Chavín iconography (materials in the collection of Manuel Chávez Ballón).

The sharply beveled or squared rims which are so characteristic of both Shakimu components are also typical of the full range of Chavín-influenced ceramic styles. They are particularly noticeable in Ocucaje 3, or Cerillos in Wallace's terminology (Wallace 1962: Fig. 3; Menzel, Rowe, and Dawson 1964: Fig. 10), and appear also in the Early Horizon complexes of the south highlands which are lacking specifically Chavín influences. The parallels in rim profile between Shakimu and both Chiripa (Bennett 1936: Figs. 27a, b, m, o; 28i) and Qaluyu (Karen Mohr Chavez, personal communication 1970) are marked.

I have mentioned that the appearance of four exotic vessel forms with excised decoration defines the transition from Tutishcainyo to Early Shakimu, and have identified bowls identical to the two most common intrusive forms. These ceramic cognates are typical of Kotosh Kotosh, and continue to be characteristic of Kotosh Chavín, being common for the type Kotosh Well Polished (Izumi and Sono 1963: Pls. 126.2–4, 13; 128.1–5). They are characteristic of a wide range of other ceramic complexes at the point of strongest Chavín influence (Menzel, Rowe, and Dawson 1964: Fig. 9b; Tello 1956: Fig. 11-n; Engel 1956: Fig. 11 E; Collier 1955: Fig. 67 b, f; Izumi and Terada 1966: Pl. 26.22–4; Willey and Corbett 1954: Pl. 7e). There is thus indication of a close historical relationship between these two vessel forms and the Chavín art style. It is noteworthy that one vessel of one of these two forms from the Kotosh Kotosh Period bears a feline design which is already strongly Chavín in detail, though executed in the techniques of Kotosh Grooved, the diagnostic ceramic type of the Kotosh Kotosh Period (Izumi and Sono 1963: Pls. 135.1; 57b.7–12). These Chavín Horizon bowl forms are manifested again in a remarkable series of stone bowls encountered by Pedro Rojas Ponce at Huayurco, near the bend of the Marañón. The elaborate, excised designs on these magnificently sculptured specimens are close to those of Early Shakimu bowls. There is a distinct possibility that these typically Chavín bowl forms ultimately have a Mesoamerican origin along with certain other features of Kotosh Kotosh and Chavín (Coe and Flannery 1967: Fig. 8; Flannery 1968: Figs. 2, 3; Coe 1962, 1963; Dixon 1959: Fig. 1d; Lathrap 1966).

This is not the place for a review of all carbon-14 dates relating to Chavín. It is enough to note that their general range is strongly supportive of the acceptability of the Early Shakimu date 650 B.C. ± 100.

So far I have argued for a particular alignment of the early part of the Central Ucayali sequence with the Kotosh and coastal Ecuador sequences and with the general chronological organization for the Central Andes proposed by Rowe. The discussion has also indicated the existence of intensive and continuing cultural contact among these three areas, but up to this point I have largely avoided the question of the nature of the culture contacts involved and the direction in which particular culture elements were moving. Now some tentative attempts to answer these questions seem justified.

At the outset and for reasons that have been discussed elsewhere (Lathrap 1967; Bischof 1967; Coe 1967), it is necessary to indicate my complete rejection of the hypotheses offered by Meggers, Evans, and Estrada (1965) that the Valdivia ceramic tradition of coastal Ecuador represents a direct introduction of the ceramic arts from southern Japan and that Valdivia was then the fountainhead out of which all of the other early ceramic traditions of South America were directly derived. In the first place, available evidence indicates that Puerto Hormiga is older than Valdivia (Reichel-Dolmatoff 1965). In the second place, there is simply not enough time between 2700 B.C. and 2000 B.C. for the direct derivation from a single source of such diverse ceramic traditions as Canapote (Bischof 1966), Rancho Peludo (Rouse and Cruxent 1963), Momíl Ia (G. and A. Reichel-Dolmatoff 1956), Early Tutishcainyo, Kotosh Waira-jirca, La Florida (Lanning 1967: 91), and Hacha (Lanning 1967: 83–4).

It is perhaps most important to examine the nature of the relationship between Kotosh Waira-jirca and Early Tutishcainyo, since even the most divergent opinions—such as mine and those of Meggers and Evans (1968: 88–92; Meggers, Evans, and Estrada 1965: 176)—agree that the similarities are close and historically significant. Meggers and Evans (1961) have suggested that Early Tutishcainyo is a rather direct derivative from Kotosh Waira-jirca or some other similar highland culture. They believe that people bearing such a culture entered the tropical forest from the highlands and rapidly deteriorated. I find it more probable that Kotosh Waira-jirca represents a blending of two distinct cultural traditions, one of which was very like Early Tutishcainyo, and relates to an upward expansion of Tropical Forest peoples to the eastern slopes of the Andes; the other of these traditions appears to be indigenous to the Central Andes or Peruvian coast. I will review the evidence which I find supportive of my position.

We have already noted that zoned incised designs are typically associated with sharply carinated vessel forms in both Kotosh Waira-jirca and Early Tutishcainyo. We have also seen that all of the carinated forms of Kotosh Waira-jirca which bear zoned incised designs have plausible prototypes in Early Tutishcainyo. The reverse is not true. There are several Early Tutishcainyo vessel forms—including two of the most important ones, the cup and the shallow carinated bowl—which have no conceivable prototypes in Kotosh Waira-jirca.

Whereas the tradition of zone-hatched, crusted decoration is the dominant--indeed almost the only—decorative tradition in Early Tutishcainyo, Kotosh Waira-jirca shows a second, completely disparate decorative tradition. This style of pattern-burnished or shallow-incised designs shows a very high correlation with a single vessel form: the large, neckless olla, with internally thickened, comma-shaped rim. The motifs of this decorative tradition are limited, consisting of arcades or triangles pendent to the vessel rim. Ceramic complexes in which neckless ollas from the exclusive or nearly exclusive vessel category have been recognized by Lanning at a number of sites along the north-central and central Peruvian coast (Lanning n.d; 1967: 85); these complexes are among the earliest so far recognized, often directly replacing the non-ceramic agricultural complexes. That part of the Kotosh Waira-jirca ceramic vocabulary which has no antecedents in something like Early Tutishcainyo appears to belong to this neckless olla tradition. If Early Tutishcainyo were directly derived from Kotosh Waira-jirca, it is rather odd that no hint of this neckless olla tradition, which includes nearly half of the ceramics manufactured by the Kotosh Waira-jirca peoples, is to be noted in Early Tutishcainyo. It is more logical to explain Kotosh Waira-jirca as the result of a Type A3 culture contact situation (Lathrap, ed., 1956) between a site unit intrusion of a culture very like Early Tutishcainyo and a community of people who were bearers of the neckless olla tradition. Much more work needs to be done, but the presently available evidence is far more supportive of the position of Tello, as well as of Sauer (1952), than it is of Meggers and Evans. The earliest sedentary communities with elaborate masonry structures so far discovered in the Central Andean highlands appear influenced by, and indeed partially derived from, Tropical Forest peoples.

By Early Horizon times the flow of cultural influence was clearly in the opposite direction. Shakimu is basically an extension of the Tutishcainyo tradition, but it is modified by exotic elements which are clearly part of that poorly understood homogenizing of Central Andean cultures associated with the spread of Chavín art. It is probably not accidental that at least one of the elements in a complex Early Shakimu design

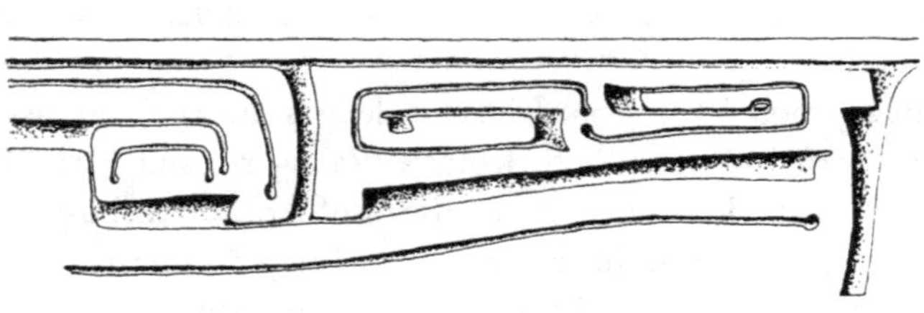

Fig. 16 *Excised design from Early Shakimu bowl.*

might be decoded as an eye in Chavín iconography (Fig. 16). Though accepting influence from the Central Andes, the people responsible for Shakimu culture apparently had a fairly complex society, if one can judge by the elaboration and excellence of their ceramic style. What is most certain is that during Early Horizon times the *selva* of eastern Peru was included in the same general "interaction sphere" as most of the rest of Peru.

The problem of a cultural interpretation of the similarities between the Central Ucayali sequence and the Early Formative sequence on the coast of Ecuador is more difficult. We have already noted that there are certain similarities in the basic vocabulary of vessel shapes particularly evident in the "cup" form of Early Tutishcainyo and Valdivia form 11. The similarities are general rather than precise, and, if historically meaningful, might be considered as evidence of a very early common heritage shared by the two complexes.

We have seen how the evolution of Valdivia B into Valdivia C and on through D into Machalilla is characterized by the ever-increasing importance of sharply carinated vessels. The evidence from Yarinacocha indicates that complexes with an insistence on carination occur very early in the Peruvian Montaña, probably sufficiently early to be the source of this influence. Michael Harner has conducted important excavations in the Ecuadorian Montaña, in what is now Jívaro country. The collections have not been fully analyzed, but it is clear that some of the materials are related to the Tutishcainyo tradition in both form and decoration, particularly to Late Tutishcainyo. A number of features of vessel form and decoration from the Ecuadorian Montaña near Macas described by G. H. S. Bushnell (1946) suggest affinities with Late Tutishcainyo, and the Yasuní ceramics from as far north as the Río Napo still show some affinities with Late Tutishcainyo (Evans and Meggers 1968: 90). In other words, the broad area of the Montaña between Yarinacocha and the Ecuadorian Andes was apparently occupied by cultures related to the Tutishcainyo tradition; there is no reason why the fluvial part of this environment should not have been occupied very early.

If the hypothesis of Montaña influence on the later part of the Valdivia sequence has any merit, a generalized diffusion through trade rather than a site unit intrusion seems indicated since there are far more continuities than novelties as the coastal Ecuadorian sequence unfolds.

The most striking parallels between the two areas are between Late Tutishcainyo and Machalilla. While the Late Tutishcainyo-like traits in Machalilla cannot be explained in terms of an invasion, they at least suggest intensive contact between coastal Ecuador and the Peruvian and Ecuadorian Montaña during the latter half of the second millennium B.C. Double-spout-and-bridge bottles, which evolve into stirrup-spout bottles in Machalilla, have a greater antiquity in the Montaña than on the coast, and the flow of cultural influence would appear to have been westward in this instance. The emphasis on carinations with an added ridge of clay, as in Ayangue Incised form 5 (Meggers, Evans, and Estrada 1965: Fig. 73) appears to be derived from the shorter forms of basal flange so common in the Tutishcainyo tradition. Here again there is the suggestion that the peoples of the Montaña seem to have been influencing the peoples of the coast. On the other hand, prefired red slip and prefired zoned red painting would appear to have a far greater antiquity on the coast of Ecuador, and may well have been brought to the Central Ucayali by the Sanidine Tempered trade ware which was probably made in the southern Ecuadorian or northern Peruvian Andes.

It is worth stressing that, in spite of the statement of Meggars, Evans, and Estrada to the contrary (1965: 176), the close similarities shared by Late Tutishcainyo and Machalilla have no parallel in the Kotosh materials, except for the ridged tops of Kotosh Kotosh bottles (Izumi and Sono 1963: Pls. 132.16, 20; 133.8). Kotosh cannot possibly have served as an intermediary for all of the mutual influence between the two areas. I suggest that the evidence indicates that coastal Ecuador and the Montaña were connected in a complex network of cultural interaction, "an interaction sphere" in Midwestern terminology, during the latter half of the second millennium. The collapse of this network in the early half of the first millennium B.C. would appear to relate to the emergence of the Chavín Horizon and its network of mutual influence in Peru and to the coeval development of close cultural ties between coastal Ecuador and Mesoamerica. Thus there was a complete shift in prestige centers and sources of cultural influence.

I have reviewed evidence relevant to the dating of the Tutishcainyo tradition, and have also shown extensive evidence for a high degree of cultural interaction between these early Tropical Forest cultures and the early ceramic cultures of Peru and Ecuador. This discussion has not provided any clues as to the origins of Early Tutishcainyo. Indeed, it has been demonstrated that Early Tutishcainyo cannot have been derived from any known culture of Peru or Ecuador. Since the transition from hunting and gathering societies without ceramics to agricultural societies, first without and then with ceramics, is reasonably well-documented from a number of places in coastal and highland Peru (Bird 1948; Patterson and Lanning 1964; Cardich 1964), it is increasingly unlikely that a source for Early Tutishcainyo will be discovered in the highland or coastal region of the Central Andes.

Early Tutishcainyo, with its complex vocabulary of shapes, its reasonably high level of technological sophistication, and its highly standardized rules of decoration, is clearly a long way from the beginnings of pottery. I would suggest that the only regions where we are likely to find its antecedents are in the flood plains on the major rivers of the tropical forests of South America.

In summary, during the period between 2000 B.C. and 1000 B.C., when the cultural pattern we call Chavín was crystalizing, the ceramics of the Peruvian Montaña were somewhat more varied and colorful than those of the Peruvian coast. The earliest of these styles already had designs organized on the modular width principle, and employed the jaguar motif: two of the essential elements of Chavín style (Fig. 17). If about one percent of the pottery used by the Early Tutishcainyo peoples and fully five percent of all pottery used by the Late Tutishcainyo peoples was made in the southern Andes of Ecuador or northern Andes of Peru, then the trade routes must have been wide open and there must also have been a westward flux of Tropical Forest ideas and materials. Once we have recognized this situation, it becomes less profitable to ask, "Were the origins of Chavín in a Tropical Forest Culture or in a Highland Culture?" and more profitable to observe that, at the time of the emergence of Chavín as a pattern, the cultures of the eastern highlands and the lowland jungles were not yet fully differentiated, and were in a demonstrable sense still part of the same culture area or "interaction sphere."

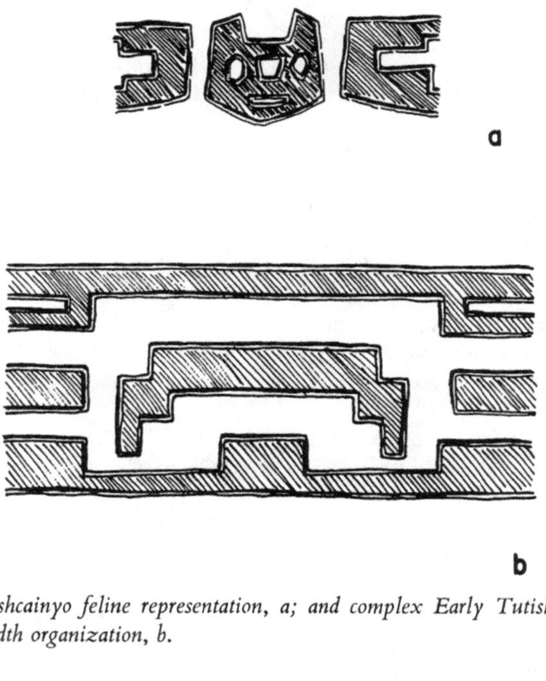

Fig. 17 *Early Tutishcainyo feline representation, a; and complex Early Tutishcainyo design with modular width organization, b.*

ACKNOWLEDGMENTS The final version of Figs. 5–7, 10, 12, 14, 17 are by Mrs. Doris Hazard; Figs. 4, 8, 9, 13, 18 by Miss Cherie Bohat; and Figs. 3 and 11 by the author.

BIBLIOGRAPHY

ALLEN, WILLIAM L.

n.d. A Ceramic Sequence from the Alto Pachitea, Peru. (Unpublished Ph.D. dissertation, 1968.) University of Illinois, Urbana.

BENNETT, WENDELL C.

1936 Excavations in Bolivia. *Anthropological Papers of the American Museum of Natural History*, vol. XXXV, part IV. New York.

BIRD, JUNIUS B.

1948 Preceramic Cultures in Chicama and Virú. *In* A Reappraisal of Peruvian Archaeology. *Memoirs of the Society for American Archaeology*, no. 4, pp. 21–28. Menasha.

BISCHOF, HENNING

1966 Canapote—an Early Ceramic Site in Northern Colombia. Preliminary Report. *XXXVI Congreso Internacional de Americanistas*, vol. 1, pp. 483–491. Sevilla.

1967 *Review of* Early Formative Period of Coastal Ecuador: The Valdivia and Machalilla Phases, by Meggers, Evans, and Estrada. *American Journal of Archaeology*, vol. 71, no. 2, pp. 216–219. Princeton.

BUSHNELL, G. H. S.

1946 An Archaeological Collection from Macas, on the Eastern Slopes of the Ecuadorian Andes. *Man*, vol. 46, no. 2, pp. 2–6. London.

CARDICH, AUGUSTO

1964 Lauricocha, Fundamentos para una Prehistoria de los Andes Centrales. *Studia Praehistórica*, vol. III. Centro Argentino de Estudios Prehistóricos, Buenos Aires.

COE, MICHAEL D.

1962 An Olmec Design on an Early Peruvian Vessel. *American Antiquity*, vol. 27, no. 4, pp. 579–580. Salt Lake City,

1963 Olmec and Chavín: Rejoinder to Lanning. *American Antiquity*, vol. 29, no. 1, pp. 101–104. Salt Lake City.

1967 Directions of Cultural Diffusion. *Science*, vol. 155, no. 3759, pp. 185–186. Washington.

COE, MICHAEL D. and KENT V. FLANNERY

1967 Early Cultures and Human Ecology in South Coastal Guatemala. *Smithsonian Contributions to Anthropology*, vol. 3, Washington.

COLLIER, DONALD

1955 Cultural Chronology and Change as Reflected in the Ceramics of the Virú Valley, Peru. *Fieldiana: Anthropology*, vol. 43. Chicago.

DIXON, KEITH A.

1959 Ceramics from Two Preclassic Periods at Chiapa de Corzo, Chiapas, Mexico. *Papers of the New World Archaeological Foundation*, no. 5, Publication no. 4. Orinda.

ENGEL, FRÉDÉRIC

1956 Curayacu—a Chavinoid Site. *Archaeology*, vol. 9, no. 2, pp. 98–105. Brattleboro.

EVANS, CLIFFORD and BETTY J. MEGGERS

1960 Archeological Investigations in British Guiana. *Bureau of American Ethnology, Bulletin 177*. Washington.

1968 Archeological Investigations on the Rio Napo, Eastern Ecuador. *Smithsonian Contributions to Anthropology*, vol. 6. Washington.

FLANNERY, KENT V.

1968 The Olmec and the Valley of Oaxaca: A Model for Inter-regional Interaction in Formative Times. *In* Dumbarton Oaks Conference on the Olmec, pp. 79–117. Dumbarton Oaks Research Library and Collection, Washington.

GROSSMAN, MARY LOUISE and JOHN HAMLET

1964 Birds of Prey of the World. New York.

HILBERT, PETER PAUL

1968 Archäologische Untersuchungen am Mittleren Amazonas. *Marburger Studien zur Völkerkunde*, vol. 1. Berlin.

IZUMI, SEIICHI and TOSHIHIKO SONO

1963 Andes 2. Excavations at Kotosh, Peru, 1960. Tokyo.

IZUMI, SEIICHI and KAZUO TERADA

1966 Andes 3. Excavations at Pechiche and Garbanzal, Tumbes Valley, Peru, 1960. Tokyo.

LANNING, EDWARD P.

1967 Peru Before the Incas. Englewood Cliffs, New Jersey.

n.d. Chronological and Cultural Relationships of Early Pottery Styles in Ancient Peru. (Unpublished Ph.D. dissertation, 1960.) University of California, Berkeley.

LATHRAP, DONALD W.

1958 The Cultural Sequence at Yarinacocha, Eastern Peru. *American Antiquity*, vol. 23, no. 4, pp. 379–388. Salt Lake City.

1966 Relationships between Mesoamerica and the Andean Areas. *In* Handbook of Middle American Indians, vol. 4, pp. 265–276. University of Texas Press, Austin.

1967 *Review of* Early Formative Period of Coastal Ecuador: The Valdivia and Machalilla Phases, by Meggers, Evans, and Estrada. *American Anthropologist*, vol. 69, no. 1, pp. 96–98. Menasha.

1968 Aboriginal Occupation and Changes in River Channel on the Central Ucayali, Peru. *American Antiquity*, vol. 33, no. 1, pp. 62–79. Salt Lake City.

n.d.a Yarinacocha: Stratigraphic Excavations in the Peruvian Montaña. (Unpublished Ph.D. dissertation, 1962.) Harvard University, Cambridge.

n.d.b Report on the Continuing Program of Research on the Culture History of the Upper Amazon Basin. (Mimeographed, 1967.) Department of Anthropology, University of Illinois, Urbana.

LATHRAP, DONALD W., ed.

1956 An Archaeological Classification of Culture Contact Situations. *In* Seminars in Archaeology: 1955. *Memoirs of the Society for American Archaeology*, no. 11, pp. 1–30. Salt Lake City.

MEGGERS, BETTY J. and CLIFFORD EVANS

1961 An Experimental Formulation of Horizon Styles in the Tropical Forest Area of South America. *In* Essays in Pre-Columbian Art and Archaeology, by S. K. Lothrop *et al.*, pp. 372–388. Harvard University Press, Cambridge.

MEGGERS, BETTY J., CLIFFORD EVANS, and EMILIO ESTRADA

1965 Early Formative Period of Coastal Ecuador: The Valdivia and Machalilla Phases. *Smithsonian Contributions to Anthropology*, vol. 1. Washington.

MENZEL, DOROTHY, JOHN H. ROWE, and LAWRENCE E. DAWSON
1964 The Paracas Pottery of Ica: A Study in Style and Time. *University of California Publications in American Archaeology and Ethnology*, vol. 50. Berkeley and Los Angeles.

PATTERSON, THOMAS C.
1966 Pattern and Process in the Early Intermediate Period Pottery of the Central Coast of Peru. *University of California Publications in Anthropology*, vol. 3. Berkeley.

PATTERSON, THOMAS C. and EDWARD P. LANNING
1964 Changing settlement patterns on the central Peruvian coast. *Ñawpa Pacha*, no. 2, pp. 113–123. Institute of Andean Studies, Berkeley.

REICHEL-DOLMATOFF, GERARDO
1965 Excavaciones arqueológicas en Puerto Hormiga (Departamento de Bolivar). *Antrolopogia 2*. Universidad de los Andes, Bogotá.

REICHEL-DOLMATOFF, GERARDO and ALICIA
1956 Momil: Excavaciones en el Río Sinú. *Revista Colombiana de Antropología*, vol. 5, pp. 111–333. Bogotá.

ROUSE, IRVING and JOSÉ MARÍA CRUXENT
1963 Venezuelan Archaeology. *Caribbean Series*, 6. Yale University Press, New Haven.

ROWE, JOHN HOWLAND
1960 Cultural Unity and Diversification in Peruvian Archaeology. *In* Men and Cultures; Selected Papers of the Fifth International Congress of Anthropological and Ethnological Sciences, pp. 627–631. University of Pennsylvania, Philadelphia.
1962 Chavín Art: An Inquiry into its Form and Meaning. The Museum of Primitive Art, New York.

SAUER, CARL O.
1952 Agricultural Origins and Dispersals. American Geographical Society, New York.

TELLO, JULIO C.
1943 Discovery of the Chavín Culture in Peru. *American Antiquity*, vol. 9, no. 1, pp. 135–160. Menasha.
1956 Arqueología del Valle de Casma. Culturas: Chavín, Santa o Huaylas Yunga u Sub-Chimú. Publicación Antropológica del Archivo "Julio C. Tello" de la Universidad Nacional Mayor de San Marcos, vol. I. Lima.
1960 Chavín. Cultura matriz de la civilización andina. Primera parte. Publicación Antropológica del Archivo "Julio C. Tello" de la Universidad Nacional Mayor de San Marcos, vol. II. Lima.

WALLACE, DWIGHT T.
1962 Cerrillos, an Early Paracas Site in Ica, Peru. *American Antiquity*, vol. 27, no. 3, pp. 303–314. Salt Lake City.

WILLEY, GORDON R.
1951 The Chavín problem: a Review and Critique. *Southwestern Journal of Anthropology*, vol. 7, no. 2, pp. 103–144. Albuquerque.

WILLEY, GORDON R. and JOHN M. CORBETT
1954 Early Ancón and Early Supé Culture: Chavín Horizon Sites on the Central Peruvian Coast. *Columbia Studies in Archeology and Ethnology*, vol. III. New York.

YACOVLEFF, EUGENIO
1932 Las Falcónidas en el arte y en las creencias de los antiguos peruanos. *Revista del Museo Nacional*, vol. I, no. I, pp. 33–111. Lima.

*The Influence of Chavín Art on Later Styles**

JOHN HOWLAND ROWE
UNIVERSITY OF CALIFORNIA, BERKELEY

CHAVÍN art is found distributed over a considerable area of north and central Peru in the Early Horizon. It is primarily a religious art in which mythical beings are depicted. Even when the mythical being is a natural animal, such as a hawk, a jaguar, or a cayman, it is provided with non-natural attributes which distinguish it from ordinary animals; for example, mythical hawks have feline mouths. On pottery and small objects, mythical beings are often shown in highly abbreviated forms, or single details from the more elaborate mythical representations may be used as decorative motifs.

In later art styles, two kinds of Chavín influence can be traced. One is archaism; that is, the direct imitation by later craftsmen of objects decorated in the Chavín style; the other is the transmission of certain Chavín conventions to later styles as persistent elements of changing artistic traditions. These two kinds of influence can most conveniently be discussed separately.

ARCHAISM

Archaistic imitation of Chavín art can so far be traced only in pottery, involving abbreviated representations of mythical beings and sometimes shape features as well. Archaism was a recurrent feature of the north coast pottery tradition, and all the known examples of later pieces imitating Chavín probably come from that area, since the one imitation Chavín vessel known to have been found on the central coast seems to be a trade piece.

The local variant of the Chavín style on the north coast is the style called Cupisnique. Beginning in the later part of the Early Horizon, the Cupisnique style was succeeded by styles quite different in nature and probably originating in other areas: Tembladera, which is related to late Chavín and also to the Paracas style of the south; Salinar, a style characterized by white-on-red painting, which probably also has southern origins; and Gallinazo, a style characterized by resist painting with organic black pigment which

Fig. 1 *Moche III jar with archaistic design; height 24.2 cm. Moche, Site F, Grave 10.* Robert H. Lowie Museum of Anthropology, University of California, Berkeley, 4-2896a. Photograph Eugene R. Prince.

seems to have had its center of dispersal in the Santa Valley and the sierra of Ancash. Then, in a kind of revival of local initiative, there arose the Moche style with its home on the north coast itself.

In some respects, the Moche style resembles Cupisnique more than do any of the intervening styles. The resemblances are most notable in the more elaborate pottery vessels, especially stirrup-spout bottles. We find similarly proportioned stirrup spouts, high polish, and naturalistic modeling reappearing after a long interval. The appearance of these older features in the first phase of the Moche style may represent archaism of a generalized sort, but I do not know of any Moche I specimens decorated with imitation Chavín designs. There are two Moche I specimens which were attributed by Julio C. Tello to the Chavín style; these specimens, however, depict mythical beings without known Chavín antecedents, and the attribution is in error (Tello 1929: Figs. 75, 76).

Archaistic imitation of Cupisnique pottery was particularly characteristic of the Moche III phase, and at least twelve examples of Moche III vessels with imitation Chavín designs are known. Three of the archaistic pieces have burial associations, and two of these, from the same burial, form a pair of nearly identical vessels. Among the unassociated specimens there are a pair and two sets of three, in some cases perhaps representing vessels made in the same mold.

Fig. 2 *Moche III jar with archaistic design; height 23.5 cm. Moche, Site F, Grave 10. This vessel forms a pair with the one shown in Fig. 1; the design shown is that on the opposite side.* Robert H. Lowie Museum of Anthropology, University of California, Berkeley, 4–2896b. Photograph Eugene R. Prince.

Fig. 3 *Composite drawing of the design on one side of the Moche III jars illustrated in Figs. 1 and 2. The black is an organic pigment and very fugitive. It is possible that the crest and wing were also outlined in black, but no traces of black can be detected in these areas now.* Drawing by Catherine Terry Brandel.

Fig. 4 (left) *Moche III jar with a common Moche III design, from the same burial as the jars shown in Figs. 1 and 2; height 17 cm.* Robert H. Lowie Museum of Anthropology, University of California, Berkeley, 4–2895. Photograph Eugene R. Prince.

Fig. 5 (right) *Moche III stirrup-spout bottle, from the same burial as the vessels shown in Figs. 1, 2, and 4; height 24 cm.* Robert H. Lowie Museum of Anthropology, University of California, Berkeley, 4–2874. Photograph Eugene R. Prince.

Here, where we are on firm ground in talking about archaism, it may be well to review the evidence that archaism is in fact involved. In Grave F 10 at Moche, Max Uhle found two nearly identical small jars with incised and painted designs inspired by Chavín style models (Figs. 1, 2).[1] These jars have good Moche III shapes, and their designs include some Moche elements: the pigments, red, white, and organic black; the wave pattern around the rim; and the "starfish" design used as a space filler. The imitation Chavín designs show a disembodied feline head with prominent teeth (Fig. 3). Some misunderstanding of the theme is evident; the rear teeth, for example, are not attached but float in the open mouth. To document the Moche III character of the lot, I illustrate two other specimens from it (Figs. 4, 5).

In Grave F 12 Uhle found a stirrup-spout bottle decorated with an incised and painted design of a disembodied feline head, also in imitation Chavín style (Fig. 6).[2] The stirrup spout is of a good Moche III shape and has on it a painted design like that on the spout of

1. A fragment of one of the jars is shown in Kroeber 1925: Pl. 57l; and 1926: Fig. 4.
2. Kroeber 1925: Pl. 57j; 1926: Fig. 3.

Fig. 6 *Fragment of a Moche III stirrup-spout bottle with an archaistic design; height 16.8 cm. The bottom, which is missing, probably resembled those of the vessels shown in Figs. 15 and 16. Moche, Site F, Grave 12.* Robert H. Lowie Museum of Anthropology, University of California, Berkeley, 4–2980. Photograph Eugene R. Prince.

a non-archaistic bottle in the same tomb (Fig. 7).[3] The vessels in this tomb represent a somewhat later variety of Moche III than those in Grave F 10 (for a sample, see Fig. 8).

The unassociated archaistic specimens, like the associated ones, are characterized by

3. Kroeber 1925: Pl. 57h.

Fig. 7 *Moche III stirrup-spout bottle from the same burial as the vessel shown in Fig. 6 with painted designs on the stirrup spout in the same positions; height 19.8 cm.* Robert H. Lowie Museum of Anthropology, University of California, Berkeley, 4–2947. Photograph Eugene R. Prince.

the occurrence of an imitation Chavín design incised on a vessel of Moche III shape and painted with Moche III pigments. As noted, they include one pair and two sets of three, the members of each pair or set being similar enough in design so that it is quite possible that they come from the same mold. The pair comprises a bottle in the Museo Nacional de Antropología y Arqueología (Figs. 9, 10) and a piece in the Museo Rafael Larco Herrera in Lima.[4] One set of three comprises a specimen in the Museum für Völkerkunde in Berlin (Fig. 11), one in the Museo Universitario in Trujillo (Fig. 12), and one in the Musée de l'Homme in Paris (Fig. 13).[5] It is a great pity that we do not know whether or not these three bottles are from the same burial; they may be, for it is quite

4. No. 1/2920; Tello 1923: Fig. 65 (design drawing inaccurate and turned 90°); Larco Hoyle 1963: 51, Fig. 87.

5. *Berlin*: Disselhoff 1940: Fig. 4; *Trujillo*: Klein 1967: Figs. 45a and 119 (design reversed). It seems probable that the spout of the Trujillo bottle was made by a different potter from the one who executed the other two, a point of some interest if the vessel bodies were indeed made in the same mold. This observation was made by Christopher B. Donnan.

Fig. 8 *Moche III stirrup-spout bottle from the same burial as the vessels shown in Figs. 6 and 7; height 17 cm.* Robert H. Lowie Museum of Anthropology, University of California, Berkeley, 4–2956. Photograph Eugene R. Prince.

Fig. 9 (left) *Moche III stirrup-spout bottle with archaistic design; height 21.2 cm. Provenience unknown.* Museo Nacional de Antropología y Arqueología, Lima, 1/2920 (562). Photograph Dorothy Menzel.

Fig. 10 (right) *Side view of the same vessel shown in Fig. 9.* Photograph Dorothy Menzel.

common to find pairs or sets of identical or nearly identical vessels in Moche burials. The second set of three comprises two bottles in the Museo Rafael Larco Herrera in Lima and a third in the Museo Nacional de Antropología y Arqueología (Fig. 14).[6] These vessels have apparently identical incised designs but differ in the subsidiary painting around the base.

The remaining unassociated specimen is a bottle in the Museo Nacional de Antropología y Arqueología in Lima (Fig. 16).[7] It and the set of three just discussed have a

6. Larco Hoyle 1941: Figs. 24, 31; Tello 1923: Fig. 64a; and Disselhoff 1940: Fig. 8.
7. No. 1/2929; Tello 1923: Fig. 64.

Fig. 11 (left) *Moche III stirrup-spout bottle with archaistic design; height 20.5 cm. Provenience "Trujillo."* Museum für Völkerkunde, Berlin (Baessler Collection). Photograph reproduced from Schmidt, 1929: 211.

Fig. 12 (right) *Moche III stirrup-spout bottle with archaistic design.* Museo Universitario, Trujillo. Photograph Christopher B. Donnan. *This side of the vessel is probably from the same mold as the illustrated side of the similar piece in Paris (Fig. 13), while the other side, not shown here, is probably from the same mold as the illustrated side of the piece in Berlin (Fig. 11), to judge from a photograph kindly provided by Alan R. Sawyer.*

general resemblance to the bottle from Uhle's Grave F 12 in the layout of the imitation Chavín design and in the fact that they have a decorative band around the base below it. They differ in details, however.

Christopher B. Donnan has suggested to me that the disembodied feline head was reinterpreted by the Moche III potters as the head of a large fish, perhaps a mythical being. The suggestion rests on two pieces of evidence. One is the occurrence of a row of fish with gaping mouths and prominent teeth around the base of the vessel in the Museo Nacional de Antropología y Arqueología illustrated in Fig. 15. The curled up noses of

Fig. 13 (left) *Moche III stirrup-spout bottle with archaistic design*. Musée de l'Homme, Paris. Photograph reproduced from Capolavori nei secoli, 1963: 121, upper right.

Fig. 14 (right) *Tembladera-style bottle, height 32.5 cm., probably from the Pacasmayo Valley. The photograph is here reversed left for right in order to bring out the resemblances of the design to that of Figs. 11, 12, and 13*. Photograph courtesy the Museum of Primitive Art, New York (Acc. No. 67. 122).

these fish give their heads a definite resemblance to the incised archaistic head in the upper panel. The second piece of evidence is the occurrence of the small "starfish" element in front of two of the disembodied heads on the jars from Grave F 10 at Moche (Fig. 3). Donnan has investigated the contexts in which this element is used in Moche art and has found that the contexts are consistently marine ones. If the suggestion is correct, and I am inclined to think so, the Moche III potters completely misunderstood the significance of the ancient design they were imitating.

Imitation implies the existence of a model. The pieces which I am presenting as examples of archaism have sometimes been explained by postulating a persistence of the Chavín style in some other area, so that the models were contemporary with the imitations. Such a survival is not plausible, however. In the sierra of Ancash, where Chavín de Huántar is located, the Chavín style was replaced by a white-on-red style related to the Salinar of the north coast (Bennett 1944: Fig. 12). The subsequent Recuay style of the area is related to Gallinazo. Further north in Piura, the Vicús area has yielded abundant vessels in styles related to Salinar, Gallinazo, and Moche I. In other words, the available evidence suggests that the Chavín style was replaced at about the same time throughout the north.

The trend of development in the last Chavín style was toward rectilinear treatments of mythical designs and reduction of modular width; even if the Chavín tradition had

Fig. 15 (left) *Moche III stirrup-spout bottle with archaistic design. Provenience unknown.* Museo Nacional de Antropología y Arqueología, Lima. Photograph courtesy Alan R. Sawyer.

Fig. 16 (right) *Moche III stirrup-spout bottle with archaistic design; height 20 cm. Provenience unknown.* Museo Nacional de Antropología y Arqueología, Lima, 1/2929 (848). Photograph Dorothy Menzel.

survived in some backwater it could hardly have provided suitable models for the Moche III specimens we have. The designs on these vessels are curvilinear and suggest prototypes in phases of the Chavín style earlier than the latest known.

The models used were presumably actual examples of Cupisnique and Tembladera style pottery. To explain the differences among the known archaistic pieces we need to postulate at least four different models, probably not all contemporary with one another. One might postulate an accidental find made by people digging new graves in ancient cemeteries, but four or more models and at least twelve imitations suggest some deliberate collecting of antiques.

The first set of three was imitated from a Tembladera model similar to a surviving piece in the Museum of Primitive Art in New York (Fig. 14). The Tembladera piece is in a quite late Chavín style, with the teeth running up over the upper lip.

The other pieces presumably had Cupisnique models, but it is not possible to point to specific Cupisnique vessels with designs that could be the prototypes of the Moche III imitations. Only about 150 Cupisnique vessels have been illustrated, however, and most of them belong to later phases than the ones from which the models for the archaistic designs must have come. The sample is simply too small. A single-spout bottle from Chavín, however, has an incised design of the general sort being imitated, a disembodied feline head (Tello 1960: Fig. 166; cf. Bushnell 1957: Fig. 5).

I know of no archaistic pieces in the Moche IV phase, and the sample of Moche IV vessels available is so large that it is reasonable to suppose that archaism was absent or exceedingly rare in this phase.

Archaism appears again in Moche V, early in the Middle Horizon. A blackware stirrup-spout bottle with an imitation Chavín design executed in relief and incision was found in a burial dating to Middle Horizon 1B at Vista Alegre in the Lima Valley (Fig. 17).[8] In spite of its central coast provenience, it was probably made on the north coast, for it has a body of a standard Moche V shape (Cf. Schmidt 1929: 189 right and 196 right). The model for the design was some specimen like the relief-decorated bottle formerly in the Vélez López Collection (Larco Hoyle 1938–39, vol. I: Pl. III; Kubler 1962: Pl. 129 left) or one of the pieces represented by some of the relief fragments from Chavín illustrated by Tello (1960: Figs. 161–4). Another piece which can be attributed with some confidence to Moche V is a bottle with an imitation Chavín relief design in the Baessler collection, Museum für Völkerkunde, Berlin (Fig. 18). The design is a simplified version of a disembodied feline head. The feature which leads me to attribute it to Moche V is the shape of the body, which is provided with a fairly high ring base.

8. Stumer 1958: Fig. 10.

Ring bases are not found in Cupisnique and first appear in Gallinazo. The particular proportions of the vessel body and ring base on this vessel are closest to Moche V specimens (Cf. Wasserman-San Blas 1938: Fig. 87).

The latest known example of a specimen imitating Chavín is an unpublished Chimú blackware stirrup-spout bottle acquired from the William H. Kelly collection by the Lowie Museum of Anthropology at Berkeley (Figs. 19, 20). It has no provenience. According to Margaret A. Hoyt, who is doing research on the seriation of late north coast pottery, the shape of this specimen puts it in the Late Horizon or very shortly before. The design is in relief and includes decoration on the spout.

This Chimú piece has some interesting peculiarities. It has the disembodied feline head shown fullface instead of in profile, and the face is under the stirrup instead of parallel to it on the side of the vessel. The position of the face under the stirrup has no parallel in known Cupisnique vessels from Chicama, but Alan R. Sawyer has photographed good Chavín style specimens from the Lambayeque Valley which have the face in this position.

With respect to the occurrence of a fullface feline head on the Chimú bottle, we may note first of all that fullface feline heads do occur on vessels which are unquestionably in the Cupisnique style (Larco Hoyle 1941: Figs. 52a, 54, 215; 1945: 9, top right; 1946:

Fig. 17 *Moche V stirrup-spout bottle with archaistic design; height 20 cm. Vista Alegre 4, Tomb 16, Lima Valley.* Museo de Sitio, Puruchuco. Photograph Dorothy Menzel.

Fig. 18 *Moche V stirrup-spout bottle with archaistic design.* Museum für Völkerkunde, Berlin. Photograph reproduced from Disselhoff, 1940: Fig. 2. *The information about this piece in Disselhoff's text (1940) is involved in a confusion; it refers to the vessel shown in his Fig. 6.*

Pl. 64d; Tello 1921: Pl. x; 1923: Fig. 61). However, none of the known examples can be considered a good antecedent for the Chimú bottle. The best antecedent is a vessel which may itself be archaistic and which deserves a discussion here.

The piece in question is a famous blackware bottle in the Museo Nacional de Antropología y Arqueología in Lima which has often been illustrated as a typical example of elaborate Cupisnique art (Figs. 21, 22).[9] It is decorated in relief with a fullface feline head parallel to the stirrup, and the stirrup is also decorated in relief. There is punctation in the background of the design. The flatness of the relief distinguishes this piece from such unquestionable Chavín style pieces as the relief-decorated mug from Grave 21, Barbacoa A, Chicama (Larco Hoyle 1941: Fig. 63 and p. 204), and the above-noted relief decorated sherds from Chavín collected by Tello. The design has very little which is specifically Chavín about it except the use of L-shaped fangs. L-shaped fangs are a characteristic of late Chavín art, occurring, for example, on the Raimondi Stone. The Barbacoa A mug certainly belongs to an earlier phase than this.

There are, it seems to me, two possibilities. One is that relief decoration constituted a

9. Tello 1929: Fig. 67; Larco Hoyle 1941: Fig. 211; Bennett 1954: Fig. 25, etc.

Fig. 19 *Chimú style stirrup-spout bottle with archaistic design; height 20 cm. Provenience unknown.* Robert H. Lowie Museum of Anthropology, University of California, Berkeley (William H. Kelly Collection). Photograph Dorothy Menzel.

Fig. 20 *End view of the bottle illustrated in Fig. 19.* Photograph Dorothy Menzel.

Fig. 21 (left) *Probably archaistic stirrup-spout bottle in the Museo Nacional de Antropología y Arqueología, Lima. Provenience unknown.* Photograph Abraham Guillen M.

Fig. 22 (right) *End view of the bottle illustrated in Fig. 21.* Photograph Abraham Guillen M.

long tradition in Chavín style pottery making, and that the bottle in Lima simply represents a much later phase than any of the other known relief-decorated pieces in this tradition. The other possibility is that the Lima bottle is an archaistic piece, perhaps made in Middle Horizon 1, the period to which we assigned the known archaistic pieces with relief decoration. The shape of the body is of no help in this case in deciding where to place it, since the body shape and proportions are similar both to those of the Vélez López bottle, which may be genuine Cupisnique, and to the shape and proportions of some Moche V bottles. If the tradition of relief decoration did not last late enough to depict L-shaped fangs, these must have been imitated from another source.

There is another specimen, unrelated to the question of the model on which the archaistic Chimú bottle was based, which represents some problems of attribution. It is a redware stirrup-spout bottle, presumably in the Museo Rafael Larco Herrera, with an incised and painted design and some areas filled with comb markings or rouletting. The design is a row of large disembodied feline heads facing up (Larco Hoyle 1945: 9, lower right; 1941: 149 (rollout); Bennett and Bird 1960: Fig. 23, center left). This piece was accepted as genuine Cupisnique by Rafael Larco Hoyle and Wendell C. Bennett. The shape of the body suggests Moche III, however, and the design is close to Moche III archaizing designs. The problem is that the stirrup is thick and has a small arc hole, unlike the other Moche III archaistic pieces. Perhaps this specimen is merely a more extreme example of Moche III archaism with an attempt to imitate an earlier spout form.

To rectify an error of long standing, I should point out that a specimen in Berlin frequently illustrated as an example of the Chavín style is neither Chavín style nor a later imitation of Chavín. I refer to a blackware stirrup-spout bottle with conical protuberances on half the surface, while the other half is smooth (Disselhoff 1940: Fig. 6; Kutscher 1950: Pl. 78 left). The proportions of spout and body on this specimen suggest an attribution to Moche III; the alternation of conical protuberances and smooth surface is a Gallinazo feature (cf. Bennett 1939: Fig. 13f, from Grave 4A in the Gallinazo Group). The angularity of the dividing ridge between the zones is reminiscent of a Moche III shirt design.[10]

To review the subject of archaistic imitations of Chavín, there may have been a generalized archaism involved in the formation of the Moche I style, in an attempt to return to the local tradition of the north coast after a period of outside influences. If so, the models were middle and later Cupisnique vessels. A wave of more specific archaism affected the Moche III style, with imitations of several different Cupisnique versions of the disembodied feline head motif, executed for the most part in Moche III colors on Moche III shapes. The models were Cupisnique vessels with incised designs, perhaps of several different phases, and one Tembladera vessel. Archaism appears again in Moche V, a phase dating to Middle Horizon 1, an epoch noted generally for its eclectic taste. The two known examples imitate a Chavín and Cupisnique style of high relief more flamboyant than that of the pieces imitated in Moche III. The latest known archaistic piece, in a late Chimú phase, also imitates the high-relief style of Cupisnique. It could even be an imitation at second hand, via an archaistic specimen of Moche V. The people of the north coast seem to have had a persistent or recurring interest in their past and a penchant for collecting antiques which could be used as models for imitating it. The imitation of Chavín pottery was only part of a broader picture of imitating earlier styles.

It is an interesting reflection on the advances made in Peruvian archaeology in the last twenty-eight years that of the eight specimens illustrated as "so-called Chavin style" by

10. Bennett 1939: Fig. 7c. I take this opportunity to correct the attribution to me of the opinion that this piece is "middle Cupisnique?" (see Rowe 1962: caption to Fig. 41). The illustrations for the 1962 essay were selected, and the captions provided, by the staff of the Museum of Primitive Art.

Fig. 23 *Design in the Tiahuanaco style of a deity figure in Staff God pose flanked by floating angels. The design is incised on the edge of a stone lintel found in a house in Calle Linares, La Paz.* Drawing reproduced from Posnansky, 1945–58, vol. II: Fig. 140a.

Disselhoff in 1940 only two would now be acceptable as legitimate Chavín style pieces (Disselhoff 1940: Figs. 3 and 5). In 1940 there were no published associations to which reference could be made and no sound criteria by which unassociated specimens could be assigned to the Chavín style.

PERSISTENT CONVENTIONS

There are a number of conventions and ideas of Chavín religious art which are also found in the religious art of Huari and Tiahuanaco in the Middle Horizon. These conventions and ideas comprise the Staff God pose, winged or floating angels—sometimes with bird heads—and the use of crossed fangs in non-feline, non-snake faces to suggest a supernatural character. The Staff God pose is fullface with the arms outstretched and a staff or other ceremonial object in each hand. In Chavín it appears to have been used only for one particular deity, but in Huari and Tiahuanaco religious art it was used for a variety of deity figures, male and female. A floating angel is an attendant figure shown with the body more or less horizontal in the air; Chavín-style examples appear on a gold plaque in the Museo Rafael Larco Herrera, where they flank a representation of the Staff God (Rowe 1962: Fig. 27). The use of crossed fangs in non-feline, non-snake faces is a common convention in the art of Huari, but only one example of it is known from the Tiahuanaco area: a carved lintel from La Paz on which the angels are shown with crossed fangs (Fig. 23).[11] This lintel is in a slightly earlier style than other Tiahuanaco sculptures, judging from the developments in the Huari area.

The occurrence of these Chavín ideas and conventions in Huari and Tiahuanaco art poses a problem, because the Huari and Tiahuanaco styles are separated from Chavín by a time gap of eight hundred to one thousand years. In this case archaism is an unlikely

11. A stepped-nose being, common in Tiahuanaco religious art, is also depicted with crossed fangs, but in this case the whole head may be intended to be feline. See Posnansky 1945–58, vol. III: Pls. xva and xxb.

explanation, because both Huari and Tiahuanaco lie outside the area of distribution of Chavín art. Let us examine the alternate possibility, that the ideas and conventions involved were transmitted across the gap by continuous tradition. The only known styles which might have helped to carry such a continuous tradition are those of Paracas and Pucara.

The Paracas style occupied the south coast of Peru during the Early Horizon. It developed under strong Chavín influence, and a few examples of Chavín style objects have been found in Paracas associations as far south as Ica, where they represent either imports or the work of Chavín-trained craftsmen (Rowe 1962: Figs. 29 and 30). The Paracas style also had a highland distribution, quite recognizable Paracas-style specimens having been found in the Ayacucho area, near Huanta by José Casafranca and at Chupas by Luís G. Lumbreras. Paracas influence even extended as far as the Cuzco area, affecting a local style represented by the hammered gold ornaments in the Echenique Hoard.[12]

The Pucara style is best known in the northern Lake Titicaca basin, but examples of Pucara-style sculpture have been found as far apart as Livitaca, in the Department of Cuzco, and Tiahuanaco, on the Bolivian side of the lake. I have put together an argument, too complex to present here, that the Pucara style has enough resemblances to the early phases of the Nasca style to warrant dating it some time in the first three epochs of the Early Intermediate Period. The radiocarbon evidence is consistent with a placement in this range.[13]

The Staff God pose is common in Paracas pottery in Phase 8, and it appears to be applied to a variety of supernatural beings, as in Huari or Tiahuanaco, rather than to one, as in Chavín (Menzel *et al.*, 1964: Figs. 44 and 48a, c). There are other examples in Phases 9 and 10 (Menzel *et al.*, 1964: Figs. 52c and 60). However, there is no known representation of a deity with attendant angel figures. Furthermore, there are no identifiable angel figures in isolation and no otherwise human figures with bird heads. Crossed fangs are abundant in Paracas art, but in most cases they occur in feline heads. There are, however, some examples of mythical beings of human form with crossed fangs (Menzel *et al.*, 1964: Fig. 30a is the clearest example). Crossed fangs disappear, even in feline representations, after Phase 8. The situation may be summed up by saying that only some of the ideas and conventions we are tracing are represented in the available sample of the Paracas style.

The situation is similar with respect to the Pucara style. The Staff God pose is used for principal mythical beings, though these are shown leading a llama or a mythical bird

12. Tello 1942: frontispiece. The specimen was found at or near Cuzco in 1853.

13. Ralph 1959:57; P-152, P-170, P-217, P-172, P-153.

Fig. 24 (above) *Incised and painted design from a bowl in the Pucara style showing a figure in Staff God pose. Diameter of the bowl, 22 cm. The colors are black, yellow (stippling), and white on a red ground (diagonal shading).* Museo Nacional de Antropología y Arqueología, Lima, P/8425 (2). Drawing by Catherine Terry Brandel based on a rubbing and notes by J. H. Rowe.

Fig. 25 (below) *Bowl in the Pucara style with a design of two running angels height 9.5 cm., diameter 20 cm.* Museo Nacional de Antropología y Arqueología, Lima, P/8425 (48). Photograph Dorothy Menzel.

with one hand rather than holding a staff in each hand (Fig. 24).[14] I have seen no example in which a being in the Staff God pose is accompanied by angel figures, yet running figures holding staffs or other ceremonial objects are fairly common, and may represent angels in isolation (Fig. 25).[15] None of the known examples have bird attributes, however. Crossed fangs occur but are not common, even in feline representations. In Figure 25 they appear in "human" running figures.

We must conclude that neither the Paracas style nor Pucara art provides satisfactory evidence of transmitting the whole complex of Chavín ideas to later styles. On the other hand, some of these ideas are known to be present in both. We may very well be facing a problem of sampling. Many of the more elaborate mythical designs are known from only one or two pottery vessels, and it is quite possible that some of the conventions we are seeking would turn up in a larger sample. Indeed, for the Pucara style the total sample of decorated specimens available is very small, and all the ones with mythical designs are fragmentary.

Between the Pucara style and the styles of Huari and Tiahuanaco there is a long gap, and no style which might be transitional is now known. This somewhat peculiar situation leaves the Huari and Tiahuanaco styles without known immediate antecedents, and demands some discussion.

At Huari, and in the Ayacucho area generally, the Huari style was preceded by the Huarpa style which has no trace of the religious ideas and conventions of the Middle Horizon styles. It displays, on the other hand, some influences from late Nasca pottery at the end of the Early Intermediate Period. The Huari style, with its Chavín-derived features, appears as an intrusion into the local tradition. Its earliest known occurrence is in the offering deposit of Conchopata, dating to Middle Horizon 1A (Menzel 1964: 4–23, 66–7).

At Tiahuanaco the situation is somewhat less clear to me, and I have had access to less of the available data. Bennett claimed that the style preceding Classic Tiahuanaco was one which he called "Early Tiahuanaco." Instead of illustrating the Early Tiahuanaco style with excavated sherds, however, he published complete specimens from museum collections lacking any data of association. I have no choice but to assume that his Early Tiahuanaco sherds were indeed of the same style as the museum specimens he illustrated. So defined, the Early Tiahuanaco style is a peculiar one. It displays some elements of the religious style of Classic Tiahuanaco but sometimes in such a fashion that the designs suggest real misunderstanding of the mythical conventions. Many of the designs are executed in a highly abstract manner foreign to the Pucara and Classic Tiahuanaco

14. Tello 1942: Pl. xx.
15. Tello 1942: Pl. xxi.

Fig. 26 *"Incensario" in the "Early Tiahuanaco" style with an abstract painted design based on a representation of a star animal; height 15.5 cm.* Museo Nacional de Arqueología, La Paz, 77. Photograph Dorothy Menzel.

Fig. 27 *Large vase in the "Early Tiahuanaco" style with a rayed head in relief outlined by a partially misunderstood fret band; height 33.5 cm.* Museo Nacional de Arqueología, La Paz, 293. Photograph Dorothy Menzel.

styles (Fig. 26).[16] An oversize tumbler in the National Museum in La Paz provides a good example of misunderstanding of the conventions (Fig. 27). It has on it a deity face surrounded by the fret band common to Classic Tiahuanaco and Huari, a series of interlocking L-lines. On this vessel the L-lines interlock correctly in part of the band and in another part are drawn facing in the same direction without interlocking. This kind of confusion does not occur in the Middle Horizon styles, before Middle Horizon 3, or in the Pucara style, where the same design is used to mark the necks of some mythical beings.

What this confusion of the religious and mythical vocabulary suggests is that the people who made the Early Tiahuanaco pottery were trying to imitate another style which they did not fully understand. Furthermore, their models were more like Classic Tiahuanaco than like Pucara, as evidenced by the fret band around the face of the deity figure we commented on and the abstract versions of star animals which constitute the commonest "representational" designs on Early Tiahuanaco vessels. The obvious inference is that there was another style antecedent to Classic Tiahuanaco flourishing close enough to the site to be imitated there. Considering the misunderstandings, it is most unlikely that the style which served as a model for the Classic Tiahuanaco designs was at home at the site of Tiahuanaco itself.

Another argument for the existence of an unknown antecedent style can be drawn from the significant differences between the conventions employed in Huari religious art and those characteristic of Tiahuanaco in the Middle Horizon. One is the systematic use of crossed fangs to identify mythical beings in the Huari style, contrasting with their near absence in this context in Tiahuanaco art. The split-face design, common in Huari religious art from the beginning, and lacking known local antecedents, is entirely absent at Tiahuanaco, where, however, other combinations of faces and frets do occur (Menzel 1964: Fig. 12; Posnansky 1945–58, vol. III: Pls. XIIb, c and XIXb). The Huari and Tiahuanaco styles have in common very few vessel shapes and purely geometric designs. The dissimilarities suggest differential borrowing from a common source, rather than a derivation of either style from the other.

There is plenty of room in which to look for the hypothetical antecedent style. In the entire area between Huari and Tiahuanaco no style of any kind has been found which can with confidence date to the latter part of the Early Intermediate Period. This fact, of course, reflects the very limited amount of exploration which has been carried out in the southern sierra. All the local sequences in this area have serious gaps in them. It remains likely that Chavín ideas and conventions were transmitted to the Huari and Tiahuanaco styles by a continuous tradition, but we cannot follow all the steps of the tradition on the basis of the evidence now available.

16. Bennett 1934: Fig. 14.

ACKNOWLEDGMENTS It gives me great pleasure to acknowledge the assistance and suggestions received in the research for this paper from Carlos Ponce Sanginés, Gregorio Cordero Miranda, Jorge C. Muelle, Toribio Mejía Xesspe, Julio Espejo Núñez, Luís G. Lumbreras, Dorothy Menzel, Christopher B. Donnan, Margaret A. Hoyt, Larwence E. Dawson, Catherine Terry Brandel, Eugene R. Prince, Junius B. Bird, and Alan R. Sawyer. The research was supported in part by a grant from the National Science Foundation and in part by the University of California, Berkeley.

BIBLIOGRAPHY

BENNETT, WENDELL C.

1934 Excavations at Tiahuanaco. *Anthropological Papers of the American Museum of Natural History*, vol. XXXIV, part III. New York.

1939 Archaeology of the North Coast of Peru; an Account of Exploration and Excavation in Viru and Lambayeque Valleys. *Anthropological Papers of the American Museum of Natural History*, vol. XXXVII, part I. New York.

1944 The North Highlands of Peru; Excavations in the Callejón de Huaylas and at Chavín de Huántar. *Anthropological Papers of the American Museum of Natural History*, vol. 39, part 1. New York.

1954 Ancient Arts of the Andes. The Museum of Modern Art, New York.

BENNETT, WENDELL C. and JUNIUS B. BIRD

1960 Andean Culture History. (Second and revised edition.) American Museum of Natural History, Handbook Series, no. 15. New York.

BIRD, JUNIUS B.

1962 Art and Life in Old Peru: An Exhibition. *Curator*, vol. V, no. 2, pp. 145–210. New York.

BUSHNELL, GEOFFREY H. S.

1957 Peru. Ancient Peoples and Places. New York.

CAPOLAVORI NEI SECOLI

1963 Analogicamente al Messico nel Centro Americana, il Perù ha sostenuto nell' America meridionale il ruolo di protagonista. . . . Capolavori nei secoli, Enciclopedia di tutte le arti, di tutti i popoli in tutti i tempi. Vol. IX: Le arte primitive (America precolombiana, Africa, Oceania), pp. 121–136. Milan.

DISSELHOFF, HANS-DIETRICH

1940 Sogenannte "Chavin"-Gefasse im Berliner Museum für Völkerkunde. *Baessler-Archiv*, vol. XXIII, no. 1, pp. 19–25. Berlin.

KLEIN, OTTO

1967 La cerámica mochica; caracteres estilísticos y conceptos. *Scientia*, año XXXIII, no. 131. Valparaiso.

KROEBER, ALFRED L.

1925 The Uhle Pottery Collections from Moche. *University of California Publications in American Archaeology and Ethnology*, vol. 21, no. 5, pp. 191–234. Berkeley and London.

1926 Archaeological Explorations in Peru. Part I. Ancient Pottery from Trujillo. *Field Museum of Natural History, Anthropology, Memoirs*, vol. II, no. 1. Chicago.

KUBLER, GEORGE A.

1962 The Art and Architecture of Ancient America; the Mexican, Maya, and Andean Peoples. The Pelican History of Art. Baltimore.

KUTSCHER, GERDT

1950 Chimu; Eine altindianische Hochkultur. Berlin.

LARCO HOYLE, RAFAEL

1938–39 Los Mochicas. 2 vols. Lima.

1941 Los Cupisniques. Lima.

1945 Los Cupisniques. Sociedad Geográfica Americana. Buenos Aires.

1946 A Culture Sequence for the North Coast of Peru. *In* Handbook of South American Indians. *Bureau of American Ethnology Bulletin 143*, vol. 2, pp. 149–175. Washington.

1963 Las épocas peruanas. Lima.

MENZEL, DOROTHY

1964 Style and time in the Middle Horizon. *Ñawpa Pacha*, No. 2, pp. 1–105. Berkeley.

MENZEL, DOROTHY, JOHN H. ROWE, and LAWRENCE E. DAWSON

1964 The Paracas Pottery of Ica: A Study in Style and Time. *University of California Publications in American Archaeology and Ethnology*, vol. 50. Berkeley and Los Angeles.

POSNANSKY, ARTHUR

1945–58 Tihuanacu; la cuna del hombre americano. Tihuanacu; the Cradle of American Man. 4 vols. in 2. New York, La Paz.

RALPH, ELIZABETH

1959 University of Pennsylvania Radiocarbon Dates III. *American Journal of Science Radiocarbon Supplement*, vol. 1, pp. 45–58. New Haven.

ROWE, JOHN HOWLAND

1962 Chavín Art: An Inquiry into its Form and Meaning. The Museum of Primitive Art, New York.

1967 Form and Meaning in Chavin Art. *In* Peruvian Archaeology; Selected Readings (John H. Rowe and Dorothy Menzel, eds.), pp. 72–103. Palo Alto.

SCHMIDT, MAX

1929 Kunst und Kultur von Peru. Berlin.

STUMER, LOUIS M.

1958 Cerámica negra de estilo Maranga. *Revista del Museo Nacional*, vol. XXXVI (1957), pp. 272–289. Lima.

TELLO, JULIO C.

1921 Introducción à la historia antigua del Perú. Lima.

1923 Wira Kocha. *Inca*, vol. I, no. 1, enero-marzo, pp. 93–320; no. 3, julio-septiembre, pp. 583–606. Lima.

1929 Antiguo Perú; primera época. Lima.

1942 Origen y desarrollo de las civilizaciones prehistoricas andinas. Reimpreso de las Actas del XXVII Congreso de Americanistas de 1939. Lima.

1960 Chavín. Cultura matriz de la civilización andina. Primera parte. Publicación Antropológica del Archivo "Julio C. Tello" de la Universidad Nacional Mayor de San Marcos, vol. II. Lima.

UBBELOHDE-DOERING, HEINRICH

1952 The Art of Ancient Peru. New York.

WASSERMAN-SAN BLAS, B. J.

1938 Cerámicas del antiguo Perú de la colección Wasserman-San Blas. Buenos Aires.